The ABCs of Curriculum-Based Evaluation

The Guilford Practical Intervention in the Schools Series

Kenneth W. Merrell, Founding Editor
Sandra M. Chafouleas, Series Editor

www.guilford.com/practical

This series presents the most reader-friendly resources available in key areas of evidence-based practice in school settings. Practitioners will find trustworthy guides on effective behavioral, mental health, and academic interventions, and assessment and measurement approaches. Covering all aspects of planning, implementing, and evaluating high-quality services for students, books in the series are carefully crafted for everyday utility. Features include ready-to-use reproducibles, lay-flat binding to facilitate photocopying, appealing visual elements, and an oversized format. Recent titles have companion Web pages where purchasers can download and print the reproducible materials.

Recent Volumes

Academic and Behavior Supports for At-Risk Students: Tier 2 Interventions
Melissa Stormont, Wendy M. Reinke, Keith C. Herman, and Erica S. Lembke

RTI Applications, Volume 1: Academic and Behavioral Interventions
Matthew K. Burns, T. Chris Riley-Tillman, and Amanda M. VanDerHeyden

Coaching Students with Executive Skills Deficits
Peg Dawson and Richard Guare

Enhancing Instructional Problem Solving:
An Efficient System for Assisting Struggling Learners
John C. Begeny, Ann C. Schulte, and Kent Johnson

Clinical Interviews for Children and Adolescents, Second Edition: Assessment to Intervention
Stephanie H. McConaughy

RTI Team Building: Effective Collaboration and Data-Based Decision Making
Kelly Broxterman and Angela J. Whalen

RTI Applications, Volume 2: Assessment, Analysis, and Decision Making
T. Chris Riley-Tillman, Matthew K. Burns, and Kimberly Gibbons

Daily Behavior Report Cards: An Evidence-Based System of Assessment and Intervention
Robert J. Volpe and Gregory A. Fabiano

Assessing Intelligence in Children and Adolescents:
A Practical Guide
John H. Kranzler and Randy G. Floyd

The RTI Approach to Evaluating Learning Disabilities
Joseph F. Kovaleski, Amanda M. VanDerHeyden, and Edward S. Shapiro

Resilient Classrooms, Second Edition: Creating Healthy Environments for Learning
Beth Doll, Katherine Brehm, and Steven Zucker

The ABCs of Curriculum-Based Evaluation: A Practical Guide to Effective Decision Making
John L. Hosp, Michelle K. Hosp, Kenneth W. Howell, and Randy Allison

Curriculum-Based Assessment for Instructional Design:
Using Data to Individualize Instruction
Matthew K. Burns and David C. Parker

The ABCs of Curriculum-Based Evaluation

*A Practical Guide
to Effective Decision Making*

JOHN L. HOSP
MICHELLE K. HOSP
KENNETH W. HOWELL
RANDY ALLISON

THE GUILFORD PRESS
New York   London

© 2014 The Guilford Press
A Division of Guilford Publications, Inc.
370 Seventh Avenue, Suite 1200, New York, NY 10001
www.guilford.com

Printed in the United States of America

This book is printed on acid-free paper.

Last digit is print number: 9   8   7   6   5   4   3   2

Library of Congress Cataloging-in-Publication Data

Hosp, John L.
   The ABCs of curriculum-based evaluation : a practical guide to effective decision making /
John L. Hosp, Michelle K. Hosp, Kenneth W. Howell, Randy Allison.
      pages cm. — (The guilford practical intervention in the schools series)
   Includes bibliographical references and index.
   ISBN 978-1-4625-1352-9 (pbk.)
   1. Curriculum-based assessment.   2. Educational tests and measurements.   I. Hosp, Michelle
K.   II. Howell, Kenneth W.   III. Title.
    LB3060.32.C74H668 2014
    371.26′4—dc23

                                                                        2013041356

To the memory of Sharon Kurns,
whose collaboration, inspiration, and friendship
will long be cherished and missed

About the Authors

John L. Hosp, PhD, is Professor and Chair of the Department of Teaching and Learning at the University of Iowa. His research focuses on aspects of implementing response to intervention (RTI), including disproportionate representation of minority students in special education and aligning assessment and instruction, particularly in the areas of curriculum-based measurement (CBM) and curriculum-based evaluation (CBE). Dr. Hosp has conducted workshops nationally on reading, CBM, CBE, and RTI. He has authored more than 50 journal articles, monographs, and book chapters. His books include *The ABCs of CBM: A Practical Guide to Curriculum-Based Measurement* (with Michelle K. Hosp and Kenneth W. Howell) and *Designing and Conducting Research in Education* (with Clifford J. Drew and Michael L. Hardman).

Michelle K. Hosp, PhD, is Director of the Iowa Reading Research Center. A nationally known trainer and speaker on problem solving and the use of progress monitoring data, she has worked as a trainer with the National Center on Progress Monitoring and the National Center on Response to Intervention, and is currently on the technical review committee for the National Center on Intensive Intervention. Her research focus is on reading and data-based decision making in relation to CBM and CBE. Dr. Hosp has published articles and conducted workshops both at the state and national level.

Kenneth W. Howell, PhD, is Professor Emeritus of Special Education at Western Washington University. A former general and special education teacher and school psychologist, Dr. Howell's primary focus has been on students with learning problems and behavioral difficulties (including adjudicated youth). He has published extensively in the areas of CBE, CBM, and problem solving. His written works include professional texts, journal articles, and book chapters (among them several chapters in *Best Practices in School Psychology*). Dr. Howell has also presented extensively, delivering numerous workshops and presentations, both nationally and internationally, on topics including CBE, RTI, juvenile corrections, and social skills.

Randy Allison, MEd, EdS, is the owner of Educational Solutions, LLC, where he provides consultative services to education agencies and school districts. He also teaches at Iowa State University. Mr. Allison began his career as a school psychologist. He then joined Heartland Area Education Agency as Supervisor of School Psychology and Coordinator of Systems Supports and Educational Results, ultimately becoming the Director of Special Education. He also worked at the Iowa Department of Education as the Consultant for Data-Based Decision Making and Progress Monitoring. Mr. Allison is a coauthor of 11 book chapters or articles on problem-solving processes and RTI and has provided presentations and consultation work in these areas in more than 30 states.

Acknowledgments

There are so many people who have contributed to our thinking and practice around curriculum-based evaluation through our interactions and collaborations with them over the years that we would need to add an appendix to acknowledge them all. However, we do wish to thank Natalie Graham at The Guilford Press, whose editorial support and guidance has enabled us to see this project through to fruition. We also want to thank T. Chris Riley-Tillman, Series Editor of The Guilford Practical Intervention in the Schools Series, for his editorial feedback and challenge to create another successful book. Extended thanks go to everyone at Guilford who touched the manuscript (physically or electronically) at some point to help make it the final product you're holding. In that vein, most of the artwork throughout the book was created by Matt Borger. Without his work, the illustrations of our ideas would look more like crayon drawings than the refined products contained here.

Contents

1. What Is Curriculum-Based Evaluation and Why Should I Do It?   1

    What Will I Learn from This Book? 2
    What Should I Already Know? 2
    Some Common Terminology 3
    What Is CBE? 5
    What Is CBA? 7
    What Is CBM? 8
    How Is CBE Related to CBM? 8
    What Are the Main Advantages of CBE? 10
    Who Uses CBE? 10
    How Does CBE Relate to Problem Solving? 11
    How Does CBE Relate to Formative Assessment? 11
    How Does CBE Fit into RTI, PBIS, or MTSS? 12
    What Is the CBE Process of Inquiry? 13
    I've Heard of CBE Before; Why Does This Look Different? 14
    What about Behavior Problems? 15
    This All Looks Complicated; Is It Really Necessary? 15
    Framework for the Rest of the Book 16
        What to Expect from Each Chapter 16
        CBE Maxims 18
        Use of Terms and Examples 18
        Forms, Figures, and Tables 18
        Apology for the Jokes 19

2. Foundations of CBE   20

    Decision Making Is Not the Same as Judgment 20
        Threats to Good Judgment 23
        Rules for Good Judgment 23
    Data and Evidence Should Be Valued 24
    Students Don't Have Predetermined or Fixed Ability 25
    Focus on Alterable Variables 26

There Are Different Types of Knowledge   27
   Factual Knowledge   28
   Conceptual Knowledge   28
   Procedural Knowledge   29
   Metacognitive Knowledge   30
Confront Common Misconceptions That Influence Teaching   31
   Task Complexity Is Not the Same as Task Difficulty   31
   Practice Isn't Everything   32
   Motivation Should Be about Accomplishment More Than Completion   32
   Learning Preferences Exist; Learning Styles Don't   34
Use Varied Teaching Approaches   34
   Effective Teaching   37
   Teaching Students Who Are Experiencing Learning Problems   37
Keep an Open and Positive Outlook   39
Chapter Summary   40

3. Overview of the CBE Process of Inquiry   **41**

The CBE Process of Inquiry   41
Phase 1: Fact Finding   44
   Action 1.1: Concern about Learning   44
   Action 1.2: Define the Problem   45
   Action 1.3: Collect Existing Information   45
   Action 1.4: Summarize Information   45
   Question 1: Is There a Confirmable Problem?   46
Phase 2: Summative Decision Making   46
   Action 2.1: Generate Assumed Causes   46
   Action 2.2: Plan Assessment   46
   Action 2.3: Assess (as Needed)   47
   Action 2.4: Summarize Results   47
   Question 2: Were the Assumed Causes Verified?   47
Phase 3: Formative Decision Making   48
   Action 3.1: Write Goals   48
   Action 3.2: Design Instruction   48
   Action 3.3: Implement Instruction   48
   Action 3.4: Monitor Progress   48
   Question 3: Is the Program Working?   49
Troubleshoot   49
   Checkpoint A   49
   Checkpoint B   50
   Checkpoint C   50
   Checkpoint D   50
   Checkpoint E   50
The Rest of This Book   51

4. CBE Process Phase 1: Fact Finding   **52**

The Purpose of Phase 1: Fact Finding   52
Action 1.1: Concern about Learning   53
Action 1.2: Define the Problem   55
   Evaluating a Problem Definition   62
   Define the Criteria for Judging the Severity of the Difference   63
Action 1.3: Collect Existing Information   64
   "Where Can I Find Existing Information That Is Relevant?"   65
   Evaluation Domains   67
   "When Do I Have Enough Information to Make a Decision?"   68

Action 1.4: Summarize Information   70
Question 1: Is There a Confirmable Problem?   72
   No   72
   Yes   73
Chapter Summary   73

5. CBE Process Phase 2: Summative Decision Making   74

Some Words of Caution   74
The Purpose of Phase 2: Summative Decision Making   75
Action 2.1: Generate Assumed Causes   76
   Rules for Developing Assumed Causes   77
   An Example   79
   F.AC.T.R.   80
Action 2.2: Plan Assessment   83
Action 2.3: Assess (as Needed)   85
   Option 1: Existing Results   85
   Option 2: Reassess on Same Task   86
   Option 3: Create/Use New Instrument   87
Action 2.4: Summarize Results   89
Question 2: Were the Assumed Causes Verified?   90
   No   91
   Yes   91
Chapter Summary   91

6. CBE Process Phase 3: Formative Decision Making   92

Action 3.1: Write Goals   93
Action 3.2: Design Instruction   94
   Frequency   96
   Focus   96
   Format   96
   Size   97
   The Heart of the Flower Is the Intervention   97
Action 3.3: Implement Instruction   98
   Step 1: Present a Clear Goal/Objective for Each Lesson   98
   Step 2: Give a Reason for the Importance of Learning the Skill   99
   Step 3: Show/Demonstrate the Skill and the Criterion of Acceptable Performance   100
   Step 4: Practice the Skill with the Student   100
   Step 5: Observe the Student Performing the Skill   100
   Step 6: Provide Immediate and Explicit Feedback about the Performance   101
   Step 7: Additional Practice of the Skill   101
Action 3.4: Monitor Progress   103
   Choosing Progress Monitoring Instruments   104
   Frequency of Monitoring   105
   Graphing Student Performance   106
Chapter Summary   111

7. Troubleshooting the CBE Process   112

Checkpoint A—Action 3.4: Monitor Progress   113
   Question 1: Are the Progress Monitoring Data Graphed Correctly?   114
   Question 2: Is the Goal Appropriate and Is the Goal Line Drawn?   114
   Question 3: Are Data Collected in a Timely Manner?   116
   Question 4: Are the Right Progress Monitoring Instruments Being Used?   118

Checkpoint B—Action 3.3: Implement Instruction   118
    Step 1: Present a Clear Goal/Objective for Each Lesson   119
    Step 2: Give a Reason for the Importance of Learning the Skill   119
    Step 3: Show/Demonstrate the Skill and the Criterion of Acceptable Performance   119
    Step 4: Practice the Skill with the Student   121
    Step 5: Observe the Student Performing the Skill   121
    Step 6: Provide Immediate and Explicit Feedback about the Performance   121
    Step 7: Additional Practice of the Skill   121
Checkpoint C—Action 3.2: Design Instruction   122
    Frequency   122
    Focus   124
    Size   124
    Format   124
Checkpoint D—Action 2.1: Generate Assumed Causes   125
    (F) Fact   125
    (AC) Assumed Cause   125
    (T) Test   126
    (R) Results   126
Checkpoint E—Action 1.2: Define the Problem   126
Chapter Summary   127

8. Keeping the CBE Process Going   **130**

Developing a Plan for Using CBE   130
    Before   131
    During   133
    After   136
Hints on How to Get CBE Going   136
Hints on How to Keep CBE Going   137
Frequently Asked Questions about Planning and Conducting CBE   138
Chapter Summary   139

9. Conclusion   **140**

Glossary   **145**

Resources   **153**

References   **157**

Index   **160**

CHAPTER 1

What Is Curriculum-Based Evaluation and Why Should I Do It?

Welcome to the world of curriculum-based evaluation (hereafter referred to as CBE) and problem solving. The odds are you probably did not get here while searching for a "fun read" or a moving literary experience. But you have no doubt read or heard of (or experienced) the need for improved instructional services in critical content areas, particularly reading and math. This is especially true for groups of students at heightened risk for failure or dropout.

There are millions of students with serious skill and knowledge problems in the United States alone. These students need exceptional teaching, and educators have an increased responsibility to make informed decisions about what and how to teach them. If you are one of those educators, this is a book for you: using CBE can quickly and efficiently supply the information you need to inform your decision making. And this book explains how to use CBE!

Imagine that you found an amazingly rare penny that you want to set aside to see what it is worth. You put it in your pocket for safe keeping and absently toss it with other coins into the 5-gallon bucket of change you keep at home. Once you realize your mistake, you know you need to go through the coins in the bucket to find it. You could check out each coin until you find the right penny, but that would take too much time and you would get exhausted before you found it. Or you could use a systematic process to break down the search into more manageable parts whereby you could bypass the irrelevant parts such as looking at every nickel, dime, and quarter when you are looking for a penny. This is what CBE does. It breaks down the process of having to go through the enormous amounts (and sometimes literally piles) of information that we generate in schools and have available to us. It applies a systemic way of doing this so that remembering a complicated process is not an added layer of decision making to overwhelm you.

WHAT WILL I LEARN FROM THIS BOOK?

This book will teach you a systematic set of procedures to help you accurately and efficiently solve the learning and behavior problems your students experience. We begin by explaining the process of CBE. Then we provide and explain the specific steps you can follow when using CBE. In this first chapter, you will learn where CBE came from as well as why and when to use it (in other words, the background stuff). But after this chapter, the majority of the book focuses on direct application. We give a general overview of the CBE process and the decisions that go into it before presenting a more detailed explanation of those steps and decisions. Through it all we provide figures and examples to illustrate what we are talking about and a variety of forms and materials—the kinds of things that will be helpful for putting CBE into practice in your classroom or school. CBE is a logic system for thinking about, investigating, and making decisions about learning problems and selecting the most practical and probable solutions to address these problems. By applying what you learn in this book to your own practice, you will have the skills to solve problems of why students struggle to learn. You will also make the decisions that increase efficiency of instruction by matching *what* you teach more directly to areas of student need. You will be better equipped to assure that the time you spend on instruction is providing the intended benefits for student learning. This is more of a procedural guide than it is a textbook, so we cover the procedures more than the theoretical foundation or necessary background knowledge that can facilitate use of CBE.

WHAT SHOULD I ALREADY KNOW?

You should already have deep knowledge of the content, curriculum, and standards in the areas you are, or will be, teaching (e.g., reading, math, writing). This is called **prior knowledge**, and you will be hearing a lot about the importance of prior knowledge in this book. Prior knowledge (i.e., what a person already knows about the task *before* a lesson starts) is one of the most important determinants of how quickly we learn. It is just as important for us as educators as it is for our students.

This book is not directly about reading, math, writing, or any content area. Nor is it about an introduction to assessment. Although we provide clarification of some terms and details that are especially important or likely to be confusing, we assume that you have a foundation in your content area and in the basics of assessment. If you feel like you need to refresh your memory, go ahead and do so. We'll be here when you are ready.

(whistling)

Welcome back! This book is about the procedures of a decision-making framework for planning instruction. Even more important, it is about thinking about the problems of students who are not learning and what to do about those problems. This may mean that you will need to reconsider your current understanding of "learning problems" as well as your approaches to assessment, evaluation, and instruction. It will require you to apply that deep knowledge you have of the content area(s) you teach. We provide description of the CBE

Process of Inquiry, procedures used throughout the process, and forms and guides to help simplify the implementation of CBE. However, there are also a few terms we want to clear up so that we are on the same page (so to speak).

SOME COMMON TERMINOLOGY

In routine conversation, *measurement, testing, assessment,* and *evaluation* are thrown around and used interchangeably, as if they all mean the same thing. However, in this book—they do not! These have always referred to different ideas and actions. That is why, as professionals, we need to use such terms with precision. And, in this book, because we describe a somewhat different approach to traditional educational decision making, we need to keep our terms consistent. Therefore, for the sake of clarity, every attempt will be made to keep them straight (not by making up new terms, but by sticking to traditional meanings). So, on to some terminology.

Measurement has been defined as the assignment of numerical values to objects or events according to rules (Campbell, 1940). That was good for Campbell in 1940 and is still working fine. However, the term is often used more generically as referring to all of the various tools we use to . . . (wait for it) measure things! In education the *tools* used to measure are commonly tests, observation instruments, interviews, and review techniques (used to carefully examine records and the products of student work). We go into these approaches in more depth in just a minute.

Measurement produces numbers. Numbers are incredibly useful when summarizing quantities and qualities that would take us a long time to explain with words—for example, "That Diet Pepsi costs a lot. It costs more than that candy bar and less than that book. Its cost is closer to the candy bar, but not quite the same," versus "That Diet Pepsi will cost you $1.49." With numbers we can communicate information about a student's behavior (or the products of his behavior) in the more manageable score format. Scores let us quickly communicate about and compare things with precision, but *only* if we all agree to use the same measurement rules!

Precision and usefulness of the information depend as much on the measurement rules applied as on the tests, interviews, reviews, and observations employed. Measurement rules tell us how to assign the numbers! These rules are a big part of any procedure's *technical adequacy.* Having measures with high technical adequacy is critical for valid and reliable decision making because the scores (i.e., the measurement results) from tests, observations, record reviews, and interviews inform our thinking. Simply put, when the data used to inform your thinking are not adequate, your decisions have a greater probability of being incorrect. Therefore, do not mess with the rules! Either give and score tools as they were designed and standardized or do not use or interpret them.

Assessment is the generic term for any of the various processes employed for collecting *information.* Assessment can be accomplished with a variety of methods. For our purposes the assessment methods include:

1. Reviewing products, work samples, files and records.
2. Interviewing students, educators, peers, parents, or others.
3. Observing students and/or educators during instruction.
4. Testing to prompt performance that is not apt to occur spontaneously, or that needs to be assessed under consistent conditions.

Collectively these are called the **RIOT** procedures. Application of RIOT is discussed later in the book.

One of the most important evaluation skills is that of choosing *which* assessment **instruments** to employ for *what* purpose. Another important skill is being able to formulate a good question for which your assessments will provide an answer. The powers of data are that they allow us to answer important **assessment questions**. Of course, employing more than one assessment procedure can provide a broader and more complete view of someone's skills. However, all of the RIOT procedures might or might not contribute to a complete reading assessment or a complete social skills assessment. Therefore, giving every student the same set of tools may not be needed—and it also can be a waste of time! Comprehensive assessment need not be redundant or irrelevant. Besides, *individualized instruction* depends on *individualized assessment*.

Evaluation is a thoughtful process that requires us to integrate and make meaning of the information before us. We engage in evaluation to collect information that will help us answer the important questions we have and allow us to make better decisions about what our students need to learn, and how we will go about helping them learn it. In essence, we use evaluation to help us understand things.

During evaluation we look at all available information in order to make a data-based *decision*. So it is necessary to know what is or is not good information. Evaluation does not necessarily require us to collect more information through tests, observations, or inter-

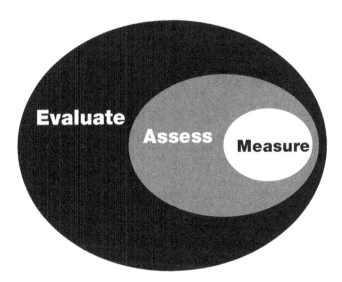

FIGURE 1.1. The relations among measurement, assessment, and evaluation.

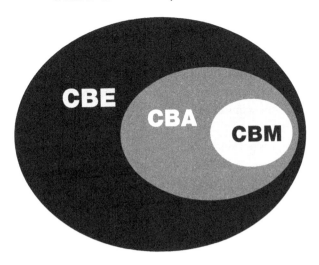

FIGURE 1.2. The relations among curriculum-based measurement (CBM), curriculum-based assessment (CBA), and curriculum-based evaluation (CBE).

views. What it does allow us to do is make informed decisions and reasonable conclusions about what all of the assessment results mean. Good assessment and evaluation only work if correctly interpreted.

Although we have presented measurement, assessment, and evaluation as different terms (because they are), they are obviously closely related. Figure 1.1 shows this relation. Measurement is one way of collecting information (albeit a very common one). This process of collecting information is assessment. The information collected via assessment is then used within a process to make decisions, that is, evaluation. So measurement is a subset of assessment is a subset of evaluation.

You are also likely to hear terms that include measurement, assessment, and evaluation that are curriculum based—*curriculum-based measurement* (CBM), *curriculum-based assessment* (CBA), and *curriculum-based evaluation* (CBE). CBM, CBA, and CBE relate in a similar way to the terms described above (see Figure 1.2). CBM (measurement) is a specific approach to measuring student performance on key skills within a content area. It is one type of approach to CBA (assessment), which is an approach to assessment that aligns the procedures and content to the content that is taught or expected to be learned (the curriculum or standards). CBA is one way of gathering information to be used within CBE. They serve different purposes, but are connected. To explain them a little more, we are going to start with a description of CBE.

WHAT IS CBE?

Curriculum-based evaluation (CBE) is an inquiry, problem-solving, and decision-making procedure. CBE was developed to help educators solve learning and behavior problems by making good decisions about *what* and *how* to teach. CBE is designed to increase the rate of student learning by grounding lessons in both efficient evaluation and effective instruction. Through an awareness and analysis of the things a student is expected to learn (i.e., the standards or objectives of the curriculum), CBE procedures allow educators to more productively understand breakdowns that occur within any teaching–learning interaction. This is done through a set of straightforward procedures for making effective "what to" and "how to" teaching decisions.

CBE helps improve instruction and student outcomes by keeping the inquiry procedure inside the classroom. It does not, for example, spend time searching for student-specific disabilities, and it uses materials and procedures taken directly from both class curriculum and instructional procedures. This is necessary for **alignment** between the curriculum and assessment and is important because classroom teachers and special educators are all concerned with students who have learning problems. Although finding students who aren't learning is easy (most educators are very good at this), it is much harder to decide exactly what to do about the problems these students are experiencing.

Educators give students a lot of tests. In fact, other than the routine accountability and grade-producing tests given to all students, almost every other test given to children today is administered because of a learning problem, and the vast majority (roughly 85%) of those learning problems are first apparent because the student does not learn/progress as expected in the curriculum. Given that the **curriculum** is the foundation of grade-level **standards** to which we are comparing student performance, the logic of using assessment that is curriculum based should be obvious. If anything, given that the presenting problem is a failure to progress in the curriculum, using measures with no relevance to the curriculum ought to be considered unconventional (if not needless).

There are so many forms of measures and assessment available today, it might be said that we are **data rich** and **data poor** at the same time. Often we collect data, but don't use it to make good data-based decisions. Part of the reason may be our limited clarity about *why* some instruments are used in the first place! A second problem is that some instruments are simply used incorrectly or employed for purposes for which they were not designed. This sort of misapplication will often render results suspect, if not meaningless, and lead to poor decisions. Think about it: If you want to know whether someone is skilled at golf, you will ask them to demonstrate golf skills and measure the number of strokes in a round of golf. You would not have them shoot basketballs, kick a football, dive off a 3-meter board, or run the quarter mile! Yet we often approach reading problems by collecting information on students' instructional needs that are unrelated to reading skills. The CBE Process of Inquiry uses direct and aligned measures of what students are expected to know.

Traditional assessment with students experiencing learning difficulties has often focused on cognitive and perceptual strengths and weaknesses, but recent emphases on evidence-based practices and alignment to standards have dictated replacing these measures with curriculum-based ones. Schools have always measured students' levels of performance in a **summative** way (i.e., after instruction has occurred). This is typically done to determine whether students meet grade-level expectations. However, many of the instruments were designed to describe these students' level of performance relative to others (i.e., they are **norm referenced**). Few are designed to examine a student's performance relative to a functional progression of skills. As a result, they have little utility when it comes to determining what a student has learned/mastered or finding what to teach next. CBE is designed to help you break down general areas of student performance (like reading or math) and examine the more specific skills and knowledge a student must master in order to meet grade-level standards. Focusing on these will have the greatest impact on learning. Therefore, CBE relies strongly on the use of CBA and particularly CBM to collect the **data** required for decisions.

WHAT IS CBA?

The term CBA is actually used in a few different ways. As we use it here, it is an approach to assessment that uses instruments that contain content either directly taken from, or very closely aligned with, a curriculum. CBA often relies on **mastery measures**—assessment instruments that contain sets of items on discrete skills that are expected to be taught within the curriculum. In this sense, it is useful and incorporated within instructional approaches such as **precision teaching** (see Johnson & Street, 2012).

The term was originally coined to refer to a specific approach, however. That has come to be known as curriculum-based assessment for instructional design (CBA-ID) because it contains direct links between assessment and intervention including a focus on acquisition rate—the rate at which a student can learn new pieces of factual knowledge (see Burns & Parker, 2014, for more information about CBA-ID).

To some, CBA-ID looks remarkably similar to CBE because both include rules for decision making and ties to instructional planning. There is certainly a good amount of overlap (they are both curriculum based, after all), but also some differences. First, CBA-ID focuses on determining a student's instructional level so that the instructional materials used are challenging, but not too difficult for the student to derive maximum benefit. This is defined in terms of accuracy on the task with specific ranges used (93–97% accuracy on reading comprehension; 70%, 85%, or 90% accuracy on drill tasks). Use of appropriate instructional materials is important in any decision-making system, but CBE also focuses on rate of performance and comparison to external standards. In this sense, CBE includes a focus on determining why a student is not learning sufficiently that can include other factors involved in the act of learning in addition to the materials used.

Second, CBA-ID relies on classroom materials for assessment (since assessment and instruction are often merged), using standardized procedures. These are sometimes referred to as **curriculum-derived** materials because they are taken directly from classroom materials (i.e., the curriculum). CBE uses a combination of classroom materials and **curriculum-independent** materials that represent the same task or skills, but that are novel to the student (i.e., there is no chance of practice effect because of differences in prior exposure to the materials). This is why CBE relies heavily on CBM.

WHAT IS CBM?

CBM is a set of consistent, evidence-based assessment procedures and the content-specific tools that use them. These tools are designed to be relevant to instruction because they offer a direct method to assess skills and when used to monitor progress provide direct information about what instruction is effective and how instruction influences the rate of learning. CBM measures are regularly composed of:

- A set of standard administration and scoring rules.
- A timing device.
- A set of materials (e.g., reading passages, sheets of math problems) that represent the contents of the curriculum.
- Explicit criteria for judging performance.
- Consistent forms and charts for recording, summarizing, and presenting/interpreting results.

Of course, to be useful, all assessment/measurement must be carried out correctly! With CBM this is not difficult because it involves tasks and processes that are already common to students in the classroom. For example, the directions are straightforward and easy to master. The tools themselves require the student to engage in tasks that are no different than those he would normally do during class (e.g., read text, write a paragraph, solve computation problems). When the student performs these tasks, he is typically timed using a stopwatch so that his level of performance can be scored in terms of both the number of responses made correctly and incorrectly per minute. Last, the student's results are charted on a graph or entered into graphic software so that trends in learning can be analyzed over time. There are a number of books and resources on CBM and the uses of CBM that are readily available and would be helpful to those unfamiliar with this assessment process (e.g., Hosp, Hosp, & Howell, 2007).

HOW IS CBE RELATED TO CBM?

CBE complements CBM's characteristics by providing validated guidelines for interpreting and using the results from the CBM tools. CBM tools are typically easy to obtain (by purchase or online) and use. Results are highly interpretable given their alignment with, and cross-referencing to, both the curriculum and instructional materials teachers use. Therefore, the impacts of teaching decisions are easily monitored through repeated CBM use. Each of these advantages makes CBM a perfect match with CBE.

Possibly the best way to understand the difference between CBM and CBE is by analogy. A longtime friend of ours named Marty used to describe the CBE–CBM relationship in terms of his golf game (at that time, Marty was trying to become a better golfer). Most everyone has experienced golf to some degree. It is rather common knowledge that the number of *strokes* in a round of golf is the measure used for describing the adequacy of a golf game. Adequate proficiency in golf is called "par." This is the expected level of performance per hole or for the total number of holes you played. The further you are *above par*, the "worse" your game is (because you needed too many strokes to complete the course). The more strokes you use, the further you are from being proficient at golf.

Marty understood that he had work to do on his game. He had already realized that simply playing more or "trying harder" was not getting him the results he wanted. So Marty decided to go to a golf pro to get help improving his golf game by taking lessons. The golf pro told Marty that the reason for his poor performance was inadequate skill on a number of factors important to playing golf well. The pro looked at Marty's grip, his backswing, his follow-through, his hip rotation, and his stance in relation to the ball (to name but a few of these important skills). After the pro's assessment and evaluation of Marty's golf game, lessons ensued. The lessons were intended to improve Marty's skills in the areas where he had problems. The lessons were not directed at all skills needed for playing golf. However, as Marty mastered more and more skills, the expectation was that his overall stroke score would go down. By improving only skills targeted by the pro, Marty hoped to get closer to par without wasting time on things he already could do well. In fact, this is what happened. Because no time was spent teaching what Marty already knew, and time was not spent trying to teach skills Marty could not learn because they were dependent on other knowledge yet to be mastered, Marty moved quickly through his lessons because they were focused at the *correct level of difficulty.*

In this scenario, Marty's golf score per game (number of strokes) was the equivalent of a CBM score. It was what we call a *general outcome measure* (GOM). GOMs reflect the many subskills needed to be proficient at some higher-level skill (in this case, the whole game of golf) without separately measuring each of these subskills. But to focus his work with Marty, the pro did a *task analysis* and subsequent instruction on the important subskills that were not adequate (Marty's grip, stance, follow-through, etc.). These were the equivalent of a CBE subskills analysis one might do for a problem with math or spelling. Marty needed these skills in order to master the game of golf. Each was important in its own right. When put together, Marty saw his number of strokes go down (closer to par), indicating that he was improving his game.

It is critical to note here that the pro did *not* have Marty work on random skills. Marty's lessons were tailored to his needs. The specific skills that Marty worked on were all necessary for a good game of golf *and* they were all alterable through instruction. It was not important to know Marty's economic status, his ethnic category, how he got to the golf course, his shoe size, or any other unrelated features. Those were not relevant, important, or meaningful to improving his golf game or teaching him the skills he was missing. This is always true of learning. Some alterable and relevant factors need to be critically considered and addressed. Others are better left alone. We talk more about this throughout the book. You will learn a lot about *alterable* and *relevant* factors that directly affect student learning in schools. We will refer to this example when presenting critical features of the CBE process of inquiry and its relation to other data collection.

WHAT ARE THE MAIN ADVANTAGES OF CBE?

As we stated earlier, identifying students who are having learning problems is easy. Most teachers are very good at this. The bigger problem is figuring out *how* to make these students successful. That is where CBE comes in. CBE is designed to pinpoint key breakdowns and determine, with increased certainty, "what" to teach and "how" to enable learning. CBE is carried out with materials directly aligned with the classroom curriculum and tools that are efficient to use. Because of this alignment, the results are directly interpretable in relation to the curriculum being taught and the instruction being used. Also, learning can be directly monitored on an ongoing basis to ensure that expected improvements are realized. Another advantage is that the CBE process of inquiry can be adjusted in depth, breadth, and sophistication depending on the nature and severity of the presenting problem (more about the CBE process of inquiry later). Another main advantage is combating something called *decision fatigue*. Have you ever noticed that at the end of the school day even simple decisions can be hard to make? It is because of a documented phenomenon where the more decisions you make, the harder it becomes to make decisions (Hosp, 2012). This is similar to how the more push-ups you do, the harder it becomes to do more push-ups—you become fatigued. A good way to ease this fatigue is by using a structured process and making the smaller decisions routine. This is what CBE does.

WHO USES CBE?

Because CBE is about making decisions to plan and evaluate instruction, anyone who needs to do these tasks could use CBE. In our experience, teachers are the ones who most often plan instruction for students—both general and special education teachers at all grade and age levels. However, being intended to make decisions particularly to solve problems with learning, often other educators are important to include in the process. This can include instructional specialists or coaches (such as math specialists or reading coaches), other itinerant specialists such as school psychologists or speech–language pathologists, and administrators and other instructional leaders. It can also be important to include the student's parents, or even the student himself (gasp!).

As you can probably tell from this exhaustive list of individuals who might set foot in a school, CBE is not necessarily a process that a single individual uses. It can be, but even when working through the process on one's own, it is important to collaborate with others, use various sources of information, and include others in the actual intervention planning, particularly if others will be responsible for implementing parts. This is one reason that we call CBE a *heuristic overlay*—the process has certain phases and actions that should be conducted, but they are general enough to be applied to a variety of content areas (academic or behavioral), grade or age levels, levels of aggregation (e.g., individual student, whole class), and individual or team applications.

HOW DOES CBE RELATE TO PROBLEM SOLVING?

We're sure you've heard of problem solving in some context or form. Quite simply, ***problem solving*** is any approach to developing solutions to problems (clears that up, doesn't it?). CBE is a systematic approach to problem solving—one that is specifically designed to aid in planning instruction for students who are having academic difficulty. It is about the thinking that underlies educational decisions. While there are many different ideas of what problem-solving processes could or should look like, most boil down to three general characteristics: ***problem identification***, ***problem analysis***, and ***problem solution*** (see Figure 1.3). Evaluation and validation is built into each stage or phase so that decisions are made based on collected information with as little inference required as possible. This is what ensures that our judgment has the highest possible chance of being good. The ultimate goal of using CBE is to maximize student learning through asking relevant questions, collecting data that are aligned with those questions, evaluating student performance and progress, and making decisions using a systematic process that compares outcomes to standards.

HOW DOES CBE RELATE TO FORMATIVE ASSESSMENT?

Another term that is gaining a lot of attention in education is ***formative assessment***, or sometimes formative evaluation. Like most terms, it is used in different ways by different people, but most agree that formative assessment is assessment *for* learning—collecting information that helps guide instruction. Formative assessment is generally folded into our instruction so that we can make continual decisions, things such as "Is Timmy paying attention?", "Can Susie do that by herself?", or "Does the class understand those directions?" All of this is information to let us know whether we need to (1) implement a behavior redirecting strategy to help Timmy, (2) provide additional guided practice for Susie, and/or (3) repeat

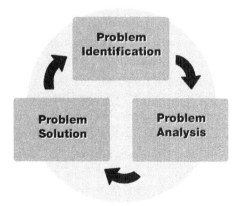

FIGURE 1.3. The three main components of any problem-solving process.

the directions. As will be evident later in this book, formative assessment is a vital component to the CBE action of implementing instruction. Formative assessment has been shown to improve student learning (Black & Wiliam, 1998) and should be considered within any instruction provided to students.

In contrast to formative assessment is **summative assessment**, or assessment *of* learning. Summative assessment generally refers to collecting information in order to summarize what a student has learned and what he has yet to learn. The information we collect has a variety of formative and summative purposes, and both are important. As we explore CBE, you will see how both summative and formative assessment are essential components of decision making.

HOW DOES CBE FIT INTO RTI, PBIS, OR MTSS?

Response to instruction or intervention (RTI), *positive behavioral interventions and supports* (PBIS), and *multi-tier systems of supports* (MTSS) are terms that are also sometimes used together. Often RTI is used to describe an academic focus, PBIS a behavioral one, and MTSS a combined academic–behavioral focus. There are some differences in their use, but all generally include several core components or features. These are usually referred to as universal screening, tiered instruction based on data-based decision making around critical components of learning, and progress monitoring. That sounds pretty easy, but what does it really mean, and where is CBE most critical?

Universal screening is used to compare each student's performance to a standard of performance that is considered to be important for future success. In essence, we are looking to see whether all students are learning, are they on track, and are they profiting from core instruction? Therefore, screening is used to make individual decisions, and to make decisions about the overall health of the core instructional program. The application of CBE in the screening process is in the analysis of student results to find common areas of problem or concern. For example, if many students are not passing the screening measure in reading or math, the question of importance would be, "What are areas of concern that are causing that problem?" In reading, is the breakdown in areas of phonological awareness, vocabulary, phonics, fluency, or comprehension? In math, is the breakdown in numeracy, facts, operations, applications, or problem solving?

Tiered instruction is applied in an MTSS approach in order to address areas that require further supplemental or intensive instruction. The important considerations at this step are "Who is not meeting the standard?", "What are the specific reasons for not meeting the standards?", and "What are we going to do to address the identified reasons for not meeting the standards?" In order to answer these questions, it is often necessary to look in more depth at the common components of the curriculum and determine where breakdowns are occurring instructionally for the group and/or for individuals. CBE addresses this process of determining the breakdowns and deciding what we are going to do about them. It provides the process of inquiry needed to determine what and how to teach in order to intervene and correct areas of deficit and concern.

Last, *progress monitoring* is used to assure that the instructional changes put in place have the intended benefit. Monitoring allows teachers to effectively and efficiently determine whether the instruction they are providing is working, and just as important, it informs teachers of the need to make instructional changes. Although CBE is not technically a part of most progress monitoring, a lack of progress in the monitoring of students may suggest the need to apply the CBE process of inquiry to better understand where instruction and intervention need to focus.

WHAT IS THE CBE PROCESS OF INQUIRY?

As we stated earlier, we consider CBE a heuristic overlay. It is a system of decision making (the heuristic) that can be applied to different content or decisions (laid over a problem). In this sense, it provides a roadmap for getting from problem to solution. Think of different ways of getting directions from your house to another location. One option is to pull out of your driveway and just start driving. Maybe you have an idea that your destination is to the west, so you head that way. You could certainly arrive at your destination, but it is unlikely that you will take the shortest or fastest route. You are more likely to take some wrong turns and the trip will be a lot longer than you needed it to be. A second option is to look at a map and plot the route. You have a general idea of how to get there—one that looks specific before you start driving. However, once you start driving you find that you have to refer back to the map for some of the specifics such as where to turn and which direction. It will be a more efficient way to get there than option one. The third option is to use a GPS. Tell it where you want to go, and it will plot out the full route from where you are now, including specific directions of where to turn and when.

Option three certainly sounds like the best one, doesn't it? For that reason, you probably expect us to equate CBE to a GPS. But it isn't. CBE is more like option two, the map. We hope this is not a surprise, but students and learning are different from roads. Roads are finite and concrete (sometimes literally). Very specific information can be input to your GPS about where roads are, how many lanes they have, what the surface is, what the speed limit is, and so forth. These are things the GPS software uses to plot your route. They are fairly consistent; but sometimes a difference arises. Construction and congestion may affect the surface, lanes, and speed. An alternate route may be needed. Again, these are finite things. Making decisions about solving educational problems is rarely that straightforward. For that matter, we consider teachers to be smarter than computers. There are a lot of things to consider when making a decision. Sometimes decision making needs to be a team process. In this way, a map is a more flexible structure for creating that plan. You can consider other sources of information such as having taken a certain road in the past, wanting to schedule stops for gas or meals, or that different roads may be more appropriate for the weather conditions. You might want to discuss this with any passengers you have. The key point is to balance efficiency (ease and speed of doing what you need to do) with effectiveness (accuracy of doing it). For educational decisions, a map lets you do this, whereas a GPS maximizes efficiency.

I'VE HEARD OF CBE BEFORE;
WHY DOES THIS LOOK DIFFERENT?

The first known sighting (citing?) of CBE was in a 1987 book by Ken Howell and Mada Kay Morehead, *Curriculum-Based Evaluation for Special and Remedial Education: A Handbook for Deciding What to Teach*. The ideas and procedures were related to prior work on diagnostic/prescriptive teaching, problem solving, and data-based decision making, but this is when it was synthesized into CBE. That text was revised two other times (Howell, Fox, & Morehead, 1993; Howell & Nolet, 2000). Through them all, you can see that, although there are advances in clarity and coverage, the process was made explicit via flowcharts that were a series of if–then decisions about exactly what to teach within a content area. Separate flowcharts were presented for each content area and in some cases even components of a content area (e.g., early literacy and reading comprehension). Over the years, these have been extensively field tested and many (possibly you) have found them extremely useful. However, there are a few reasons for the changes reflected in this book.

First, CBE was formerly applied as a sort of GPS-style system. With its relation to prescriptive teaching, CBE was created prescriptively. In this sense it provided a very clear guide for what to decide and why. When first developed and through a few revisions, this level of prescription was often necessary. The high level of content and procedural knowledge for conducting a detailed task analysis was not something that aligned with the pedagogical movements of the 1980s and 1990s and therefore teacher training. Today's teacher training provides much greater detail and therefore a greater ability to make the decisions within the framework.

Second, using a consistent process that is an overlay across various content areas is less complex for implementing CBE. Having a single procedure means it is easier to learn and apply because each use is a repetition, and as we know, more repetitions mean less time to mastery.

Third, the increasing emphasis on using methods and materials that have research demonstrating their effectiveness has led to a differentiation of some of the terms. Although we used to use such terms as *field tested* and *proven*, we now describe methods and materials as evidence based or research based. **Evidence based** means that there is rigorous, high-quality research that has examined that specific method or product. Prescriptive procedures (such as **standard treatment protocols**) require evidence-based support because specific directions for materials and strategies are included. A heuristic requires **research-based** support, meaning that there is rigorous, high-quality research that has examined some individual components to make sure that they work (e.g., use of formative assessment), and these are used without explicit mandates of when, where, and how.

Last, prescriptive approaches are usually more applicable for making decisions about one student at a time because of the explicitness of each decision. CBE has always advocated for aligning the intervention with the source of the problem (if the problem is that the information is not presented in the curriculum, it is the curriculum that needs changing rather than anything specific to a single student), but the prescriptive decisions are about individual student performance. By using a heuristic overlay approach, the same procedures can be used to make decisions about groups of students, classrooms, grade levels, and so on.

WHAT ABOUT BEHAVIOR PROBLEMS?

For those who are familiar with the previous books on CBE, you know that there were specific chapters addressing social skills and task-related behaviors. Academic and behavioral problems often go hand in hand. Just because a student is having difficulty with math computation doesn't mean that the cause of that difficulty is a lack of computation skill; it might be heightened anxiety the student is experiencing because he is being bullied. In a similar vein, a student may be acting out because of the frustration that comes from not being able to read proficiently. Because CBE is a systematic process for what needs to be taught and how it should be taught, it is generally impossible to completely separate academics and behavior. However, there is only so much space in this book. Because of differences in the details of focusing on behavior problems versus academic problems, we focus on addressing problems that are primarily academic, but will include some examples that include related behavior issues. Other resources in the Guilford Practical Intervention in the Schools Series are dedicated to addressing behavioral problems, and we refer you to those because no single resource or approach can cover all of our educational needs.

THIS ALL LOOKS COMPLICATED; IS IT REALLY NECESSARY?

It may look complicated initially, but it will make a lot of sense once you get the basic ideas and learn the CBE process of inquiry for thinking about problems. And yes, *it is very important*! Being able to assess and evaluate *what* and *how* to teach is arguably the most important part of effective instruction. Without it you may be delivering great lessons to students who already know the content, or worse, to those without the prior knowledge needed to understand the lesson. Think of the golf analogy. What if Marty was good enough to play a round of golf and consistently score an 80 when par is 72? We might imagine that he would need less problem solving and instruction than if he consistently scored 120. The bigger discrepancy between performance and the expectation (par), the more in-depth consideration and instructional effort are required for meaningful changes to occur.

The CBE process of inquiry you will be learning allows you to look deeply into problems and their solutions. In-depth evaluation of the skills required that a student does and does not have will allow you to efficiently and effectively address your students' learning needs. Also, the CBE process of inquiry is flexible. It does not need to be any more complicated and "deep" than the severity of the problem you are encountering demands. Smaller problems will likely require less analysis and inquiry. In comparison, more severe problems will require more detailed analysis, deeper understanding of the missing skills, and more specific information about what and how to teach.

FRAMEWORK FOR THE REST OF THE BOOK

Before we move on to the chapters that detail the rationale for and process of CBE, we want to provide an advance organizer to describe what it will look like and explain some of the features you will find. This book provides you with a primer on the foundations of CBE. This includes what you need to know *before* undertaking the CBE process, what you need to know and think about *during* the CBE process, and what you need to do and be aware of *after* the CBE process. It's designed to introduce you to CBE, so there will be times when you feel that the information is relatively basic or simple. This is due to the need for building a strong foundation for more complex information and tasks (as well as the amazing clarity of our writing). The introductory nature of the book also means that it is not comprehensive. We cannot provide an example or caveat for every potential concern or problem that might need to be addressed in an educational setting (imagine the size of that book). Rather, our intent is to provide a framework for decision making that you can apply to solve the problems you encounter in your professional life. The book is laid out to walk through that framework in a sequential fashion.

What to Expect from Each Chapter

- **Chapter 1.** Been there, done that. It answers all those questions you had when you first picked up the book and gives you the reasoning for why you are going to read the rest of it by placing CBE in the context of educational practice and need.

- **Chapter 2.** This chapter provides a summary of some foundational concepts of CBE. Without a consistent understanding of these foundations, the CBE process will not be as efficient or effective as it could be. There are some characteristic ways of thinking that guide what we do and why we do it. Like good instruction, we present these in an explicit manner because the greater your awareness of them and how you experience them, the more effective you will be in using CBE.

- **Chapter 3.** When building a house, carpenters need to attend to specifics of where nails, studs, and walls go, but they always have the blueprints handy for reference. This chapter is the blueprint for CBE. It gives a bird's-eye view—an overview of all the different phases, actions, and questions that make up the CBE process. When going through the rest of the book (which is more detailed), if there are times when you feel like you are getting caught up in the details, this is the chapter to review for that big picture.

- **Chapter 4.** The CBE process is divided into three distinct phases that are composed of different actions and purposes. We have broken the detail chapters out by each specific phase. This chapter details *Phase 1: Fact Finding*. Fact finding is about bringing together all the information that might be relevant for making decisions about the problem you are trying to solve—learning difficulty by a student or students you work with.

- **Chapter 5.** This chapter details *Phase 2: Summative Decision Making*. Once the facts have been collected and the problem confirmed, summative decision making is the detective work to identify why the problem is occurring from the perspective of what can be done to solve it. In our experience, this detective work is most often neglected in education. Educators are solution focused and want to be helpful, so sometimes spending the extra time to ensure that we are applying an appropriate solution gets lost in the shuffle.

- **Chapter 6.** *Phase 3: Formative Decision Making* encompasses the heart of what we as educators have been trained to do—teach! In thinking about explicit details of instruction design and implementation, this chapter also puts these tasks in the framework of the CBE process. The time spent collecting information and doing our detective work serves as the foundation for the implementation of instruction in this phase. Because there isn't enough space to give detailed descriptions of instruction or intervention in every content area at every level, we provide an overview of common characteristics and a few well-placed examples to illustrate the points.

- **Chapter 7.** Although we have been detailed in the previous three chapters that outlined the particulars of the three phases of the CBE process, and you have been very planful in your application of the CBE process to make decisions to solve educational problems, things happen. We realize that application of the CBE process, no matter how planful we are, does not always result in the outcome that we are looking for. So when this happens we have added a process for troubleshooting. Why be planful in implementing the process if you are not going to be planful in trying to determine why you didn't get the desired result? Once you have implemented CBE enough times to feel confident with the process, you might actually want to use some of the tips in this chapter for making formative decisions about the process. However, we don't recommend attempting that from the start because it adds layers of decision making and complexity. It would be like attempting a Foot Jam Endo when you were first learning how to ride a bike.

- **Chapter 8.** This chapter is a bit of a transition from the details of using the CBE process to systematic applications. Chapters 4 through 6 provide details about what you do and what questions to ask; however, there are additional "behind-the-scenes" questions that need to be answered to implement CBE. These are things like who will collect certain types of information, what materials and resources are available or need to be acquired, and what kinds of time management or scheduling are needed to ensure that we can be planful yet efficient. Chapter 8 address the school or district structures and procedures that might need to be considered for implementation of CBE.

- **Chapter 9.** This is a summary chapter that provides a conclusion to the book. It ties the details of practice and conceptual foundations together to bring you back to that big-picture blueprint. It also should serve as a motivator to reassure you that now that you have read about and learned the details of the CBE process, you can use it in your own practice.

- **Glossary, Resources, and References.** At the back of the book, you can find some additional information. First is a Glossary. This is a list of important terms throughout the book (yes, just like all glossaries). Any word or term that is both **bold** and *italicized* is included in the ***Glossary***. Next, the Resources section is a list of websites where materials and other sources are available. They are not included as references, but we feel they're pretty useful for CBE. Last, where there is a citation in the text of the book, the full reference is provided in the References section.

CBE Maxims

Throughout this book you will see various pullouts that are labeled "CBE Maxims." These are some quotes that express the essence of CBE. The reason these have been set aside is because we find that they can be useful as a set of mantras or "daily CBE affirmations." As educators, when we are fully engaged in teaching and making decisions, it is easy to lose sight of the big picture because we have to be so focused on the details. When we're in this detail-focused mind-set, it is easy to miss signs that indicate we should do something in particular or something different from what we're doing. These maxims can serve as prompts to remind us when we need to do something to help us keep the big-picture focus when mired in details, or to guide us to focus our energies on important tasks that will help us teach. Don't be afraid to print them out or write them on cards or slips of paper to place them in locations where they can be reminders (Ken had a student paint some onto little flower pots so she could keep them handy in her classroom). We each have ample experience using the CBE process, but still refer to these maxims from time to time. You will find the maxims in Chapters 2–6. In Chapter 7, the format is slightly different, in that it includes "Troubleshooting Tips" instead. They use the same format, but whereas the maxims are for key concepts in CBE, the tips are for practice.

Use of Terms and Examples

When speaking about the professionals who work in schools we will use the term "educators" rather than "teachers." This is because CBE can be useful for not just teachers, but also for other educators that can include intervention specialists, reading coaches, math coaches, instructional coaches, school psychologists, speech–language pathologists, and a whole host of others.

There are other times when we will present a specific hypothetical example. Rather than move among different teacher and student names, switching from male to female teachers and students, we are going to stick with a consistent example. When we provide a hypothetical example, we typically refer to Ms. Smedley, a second-grade teacher at Edsel Elementary. We also refer to other teachers and grade levels at Edsel when examining data aggregated to a classroom or grade level. Ms. Smedley's student who is experiencing a learning problem is Hubert.[1] You'll hear a lot about him.

Forms, Figures, and Tables

Throughout the book there are figures and tables to illustrate the concepts and strategies that we are discussing. Some will be helpful guides for your own use of data and for displaying information. Those that have lists or concepts that we felt might be handy as reference are also formated as reproducible posters. You can keep them handy for reference or post

---

[1]Ms. Smedley and Hubert are fictional characters. Any resemblance to real persons, living or dead, is purely coincidental.

them somewhere you have consistent team meetings to discuss data and decision making, such as a conference room.

We have also included a variety of reproducible forms that we find useful for organizing and guiding our thinking and doing when using CBE. Rather than include these in an appendix, where they would all be together for handy copying, they are included within the chapters where the information is discussed and they would be used at that point within the CBE process. Because of this, we know that you do not want to have to flip through the book every time you want to copy a certain form. Therefore, we recommend tabbing the pages with forms so that you can find them easily.

Apology for the Jokes

Last, throughout this book you will notice comments that you will occasionally recognize as jokes. Discussions of assessment, evaluation, and instruction can often devolve into extremely dense and dry treatments of the topic. We prefer to try to keep the mood light and the topic entertaining by interspersing some humor. Those who prefer the dense and dry texts have probably already stopped reading, so it's just us now. Let's have some fun while we learn.

CHAPTER 2

Foundations of CBE

In the previous chapter, we answered some common questions we hear about the "why" of CBE. We know you are anxious to get to the "how"—you're an educator, you're used to *doing*. It's what we educators do. However, first it's important to talk a little more about some of the key concepts that are foundational to CBE. CBE contains a lot of actions that you're used to—there's some emphasis on assessment (you're used to that) and there's a lot of emphasis on instruction (you certainly know about that too)—but it does include different actions than you might be used to. How we think determines what we do. The key concepts included in this chapter are primarily about how to think in CBE.

> **CBE MAXIM #1:**
>
> **How we think determines what we do!**

DECISION MAKING IS NOT THE SAME AS JUDGMENT

Maybe the first thing to figure out is whether these two terms are redundant. They are certainly sometimes used interchangeably. Deciding is an act (i.e., something one does), whereas judgment is a quality (i.e., how well something is done). Therefore, *judgment* can be thought of as the quality of deciding. It is possible to make a decision without good judgment. For example, Leader (1983) reported on an incident that happened during World War II. Admiral Karel Doorman of the Royal Netherlands Navy decided to engage a stronger force of the Japanese Navy. Upon encountering the enemy, he signaled "follow me" to his ships and got half of them destroyed, himself killed, and didn't sink a single enemy vessel. Doorman was decisive (and brave), but in retrospect his judgment has been questioned.

In general, if the contention (the problem we are trying to solve using the decision) gets resolved to our satisfaction, we usually think it was done with good judgment. If the resolution does not seem positive, then the judgment seems bad.

It is easier to outline steps for decision making (it's what much of this book is about), than the steps to good judgment. According to Edwards and Newman (2000), there are at least three reasons for this:

1. Judgment makes use of information, which can be seen and worked with, to draw conclusions about things that can't be seen (because they are absent or in the future, like a resolution to a problem). This is called *inference*—developing conclusions from a body of *evidence.*
2. The conclusions drawn in situations requiring inference only have a *probability* of being correct. When there is no risk of an incorrect decision, inference is not necessary and therefore judgment is a moot point.
3. Good or bad judgment is defined by how well it matches the inference needed and whether the outcome is good or bad. (Joking about your boss in front of your boss's best friend is probably never good judgment—even when nothing goes wrong. It is clearly bad judgment when something does go wrong.)

The word *probability* is a critical one for this discussion (and for this entire book). Some of the synonyms for probability are "chance," "likeliness," and even "odds." In teaching, few actions lead to absolute and predictable outcomes. Therefore, decisions that appear to be based on the best possible inference (i.e., good judgment) don't always work. This results from the fact that outcomes often depend on more than our decisions. Consider Admiral Doorman's unfortunate naval battle. Was it bad judgment that the admiral went after 17 Japanese ships with only 15 Allied ships? In 1797 Horatio Nelson violated British battle protocol and took on 18 enemy ships with his *single* ship. He captured two Spanish vessels, turned back the enemy fleet, and as a result was promoted to admiral (Leader, 1983). On the surface, Nelson's decision seems like worse judgment than Doorman's, but the conclusions drawn based on the available information (i.e., the inference) lead to determinations of good or bad judgment.

The definition of good judgment, then, does not hinge on good results. However, the probability of good results increases whenever our inferences are strongly supported by the evidence (i.e., logical). Good judgment reduces the risk of bad results, but it does not guarantee success.

Experts, regardless of their field, tend to work in certain characteristic ways (Laufer, 1997). As has already been pointed out, expert teachers make good use of routines, which allows them to accomplish common classroom tasks. This tendency to make the "small stuff" routine to save energy for the "big stuff" is one characteristic of experts. Experts also tend to see patterns, or themes, where novices may only see unrelated events (Carter, Cushing, Sabers, Stein, & Berliner, 1988). Experts are thought to be experts because they make the best decisions or go about making decisions very well (regardless of outcome). Their work is judicious and polished. Still, experts are not always correct, as it is not always possible to be correct. This means that experts are willing to take risks and to be accountable for their actions. Experts learn from their own experience and are keenly interested in the experiences of others.

Here is an illustration. A practicum student did a lesson in front of his university supervisor, and the lesson was a disaster. Everything went wrong. After it was over, the practicum student told the supervisor, "That was terrible; I blew the lesson." The supervisor replied, "It isn't over yet" and had the student reflect on how to improve. She asked the student if he could explain what went well, what went wrong, and develop a plan for correcting the problems for the next lesson.

As it turned out, the practicum student was able to identify specific things that went well or badly and refer to the evidence he had for making that judgment. By using what he had learned in classes and field experiences to reflect on his first lesson, he made changes to his plan for the second lesson. The second lesson was great. Even though the practicum student made errors in the planning and delivery of instruction, he was able to use information to guide his decision making and maximize his judgment.

We all make the errors described above many times a day. That's because these errors are all completely human and illustrate ways of thinking that may actually benefit us at times (Nisbett & Ross, 1980). To control these errors, we need two things. First, we need to recognize when our jobs call for work that is professional, focused, and reflective. Second, we need a set of guidelines (like the ones below) to follow when we do that kind of work. The threats to and rules for good judgment have been adapted to educational decision making and will be referred to frequently throughout the text. Read them carefully now, and review them any time you are faced with a decision about what or how to teach a student. To keep them in mind while having to make complex decisions, we recommend consulting Figure 2.1—"Rules for Good Judgment"—regularly. It can provide triggers to remind you of things to do to maximize your probability of making good decisions and is suitable for framing.

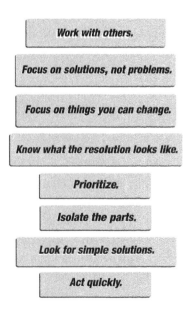

FIGURE 2.1. Rules for good judgment.

Threats to Good Judgment

In education we tend to spend most of our efforts evaluating student performance, but it is not unreasonable to occasionally turn our attention to evaluate our own professional efforts. Evaluation of our decision-making or problem-solving activities can provide us with a good deal of formative information of how our own actions influence student learning. In addition, educators are increasingly being held accountable for the quality of their performance in this critical area.

Because it is easiest to create or identify a model for bad judgment (just ask Admiral Doorman), it is important to attend to, and prepare for, some common threats to good judgment (see Table 2.1). Keeping these in mind helps raise the probability of good judgment.

Rules for Good Judgment

In addition to the threats to be aware of, there are rules to consider to improve judgment. These are additional considerations that keep us focused on important things and less likely to be drawn into the trap of one of the threats to good judgment. These include:

- *Work with others.* If possible, collaborate. Having the benefit of others' experience and knowledge can make the decision-making process more effective. If you are working through the majority of the process alone, work in opportunities to get feedback from others as appropriate.
- *Focus on solutions, not problems.* You might hear people talk about "admiring the problem." This is what happens when we get stuck in the stage of defining and validating the problem. Although it is important to do well, the most important thing is to focus on the solution to the problem. That is what will lead to better learning for the student.
- *Focus on things you can change.* Think about what the student needs to learn and things that are under your control as an educator—particularly through instruction.
- *Know what the resolution looks like.* Make sure that success is clearly defined. If our instruction is successful, what will the student be able to do, and how well will he be able to do it, once we are finished?
- *Prioritize.* Consider this problem in relation to other needs. Ones that are dangerous if not addressed or must be addressed before you can address others need to be prioritized.
- *Isolate the parts.* Determine whether the problem can be divided into smaller parts that can be solved more easily than others. This can be motivating for both the student and you because you can see progress being made toward the overall solution.
- *Look for simple solutions.* Big difficulties do not always have complex solutions. If you can find a simple solution to a part, or a way to make the overall solution easier, the entire process will be more efficient.
- *Act quickly.* The sooner you start working on the solution, the sooner a resolution will be achieved. The bigger the difficulty or the further behind the student is, the more important this becomes.

TABLE 2.1. Threats to Good Judgment

Threat	Explanation
Selective attention (confirmation bias)	Seeing what you expect, or want to see; only looking for confirming information
Primacy/recency	The first information guiding everything else you do or overreliance on the last information you receive
Premature resolution	Making a decision before enough information is collected or alternate solutions are generated/considered
Inertia in thinking	Unwillingness to change existing thinking in the face of disconfirming evidence
Salience	Things that are most common or most extreme tend to be easier to remember and therefore focused on more
Missing prior knowledge	Trying to make a decision about something you do not have enough knowledge about (often cultural, content specific, or context specific)
Misdefinition of the problem	Defining the problem too narrowly, on a trivial aspect, or not clearly enough
Lack of perspective	Only seeing things one way (e.g., not considering the parents' perspective)
Role fulfillment/ groupthink	Conforming one's decision making to others' expectations
Fear	Of failure, risk, success, responsibility, liability, or nearly anything else
Sample size	Drawing conclusions from too few experiences or examples

DATA AND EVIDENCE SHOULD BE VALUED

Decision making, inference, and judgment are all based on the information available. Just like the old computer adage "garbage in, garbage out," if we are making inferences based on poor or irrelevant information, it doesn't matter if we follow all the rules to good judgment. Even though our inferences will be well aligned with the information we based them on, they will not help us to solve the problem at hand. In fact, they are likely to create more problems by delaying appropriate intervention while we address a problem that isn't really there.

An argument that we hear occasionally (too often, really) is an educator ignoring or discrediting a source of information because they do not feel that it is "authentic" or a "good reflection of what (that student) can do." In addition to the potential threats to good judgment (such as confirmatory bias and missing prior knowledge) inherent in this concern are the concepts of content and construct evidence of validity (Messick, 1989) and reliability of the instrument. However, there are empirical ways that these concepts can and should be tested.

It is important to remember that assessment procedures are tools. Like any tool, they do the job they were designed to do, provided the operator of the tool uses them appropriately. The result that is provided is a piece of information—nothing more, nothing less. It really has no meaning until we provide it with some, which is why the reliability and validity of instruments is tested and standards are developed for using and interpreting the results.

STUDENTS DON'T HAVE PREDETERMINED OR FIXED ABILITY

It is commonly assumed that the speed and eventual extent of most learning is determined by a student's fixed ability or capacity. This idea, which is only true in extreme circumstances (and therefore rare), can have serious negative implications when it is applied often. It becomes a convenient excuse for not working even harder to help a student succeed. If a teacher is working under the assumption that she already knows what the student is capable of learning, she may continue to treat the student according to this preconception. As a result, the teacher may hold inappropriately low expectations for the student or fail to attend to displays of competence that exceed what has been predicted. These displays may even be labeled overachievement and disregarded as some sort of fluke. This is sometimes referred to as "blaming the child."

A teacher who believes that a student's capacity to learn is fixed may interpret that student's learning difficulty as evidence that the student has reached the limits of his potential. As a result, when a student starts having trouble, the teacher may give up trying to teach him (Greenwood, 1991; Teddlie, Kirby, & Stringfield, 1989). Worse, she may inadvertently teach the student to take the same view.

One of the main goals of this chapter is to convince you that students who haven't learned in the past *can* learn in the future. This is important because without that belief (and a positive outlook), the entire CBE process breaks down. Infer-

> **CBE MAXIM #2:**
>
> **Students who haven't learned in the past *can* learn in the future!**

ences will be made that are not logical conclusions from the evidence at hand. The idea that things like capacity, potential, ability, or intelligence are fixed is inconsistent with current learning theory (Ambrose et al., 2010). In fact, *students learn how to learn*. Anyone who has spent time with children at different ages knows that a preteen does not use similar learning approaches as a preschooler. In fact, you probably see growth in use of learning strategies in your students from the beginning to the end of the school year.

CBE MAXIM #3:

Students learn how to learn!

Learning is influenced by the quality of teaching, the nature of the content and tasks, and student characteristics. The student characteristics of greatest importance to a teacher are those that are alterable (Bloom, 1980). These are the skills, strategies, perceptions, expectations, and beliefs that students learn.

FOCUS ON ALTERABLE VARIABLES

A variable is a characteristic of some person, place, thing, or action that may or may not be involved in the act of learning (e.g., "student height" and "intensity of room lighting" are variables). *Alterable variables* are things that teachers can change through the process of instruction. They are sometimes called "proximal variables," as they are close to the learning event and have been shown to directly and immediately affect the quality of learning. Because we are talking about instruction or intervention here, something is considered unalterable if it can't be changed through reasonable classroom work.

Some examples of proximal variables are the student's understanding of the purpose of the lesson, the sequence and structure of the lesson, and the classroom management skills or strategies of the teacher. Student background knowledge of the topic and enabling behaviors (such as knowing how to hold a pencil or to complete an activity) are also proximal. All of these can be changed through instruction and are the result of a student's or teacher's previous learning. These are the things that teachers need to think about because these are the things that we can do something about.

The purpose of presenting this information here is to emphasize that the cognitive functions students employ in learning are not static or permanent, but can be directly improved through instruction. Student cognition is an alterable variable. We can change students' cognition (or thinking). We call that learning. It's what we as teachers do (for fun, the next time someone asks you what you do for a living tell them you are a "student cognition engineer").

So in contrast, "unalterable" variables are those that a teacher cannot reasonably be expected to change through instruction. They are sometimes called *distal* variables because, although they may affect the probability that learning will occur, they do not have a direct and immediate impact on the quality of lessons. Here are some variables that, in this sense, are considered *unalterable*: race, gender, family poverty, parental drug use, ethnicity, teachers' education, teachers' caring, class size, birth order, school funding, various student abilities (e.g., cerebral dominance, innate potential to learn), and student disability label. Although these are considered to be unalterable, some are important; they are simply beyond the influence of effective instruction. Certainly school funding, class size, and family poverty can be changed—and they should be! But that alteration won't come about through a few weeks of classroom instruction (it is more likely to occur in the voting booth). That's why, despite their importance, they are called unalterable.

It is unfortunate, but it has been found that when asked to explain why a student is having trouble in class, many teachers report that the problem is the result of unalterable variables (Ysseldyke, Algozzine, & Thurlow, 2000). This error in thinking effectively stops the teacher from engaging in productive decision making. However, teacher thoughts about teaching (like student thoughts about math) are learned. And that means that they also can be changed.

An added bonus of focusing on alterable variables is that, by definition, they can be changed. This means that we are more likely to change them when we try to (as long as we're persistent and doing something that will effect change). When we accomplish things, we feel better about what else we can change. When we focus on unalterable variables, we have lost the power to change things, and it will be frustrating. This frustration leads to lower job satisfaction and higher burnout. Aren't there enough frustrating things in your life without focusing on unalterable variables?

THERE ARE DIFFERENT TYPES OF KNOWLEDGE

Learning is influenced by the quality of teaching, the nature of tasks, and student characteristics. The student characteristics of greatest importance to a teacher are those that are alterable (Bloom, 1980). These are the skills, strategies, perceptions, expectations, and beliefs that students learn. All of these are lumped under the heading *prior knowledge.* A student's prior knowledge (what he already knows) is the primary personal limitation on his learning.

This means that the students who have developed or mastered the fewest skills have the hardest time in school. On the face of it, this seems pretty obvious. However, many people attribute difficulty in school to deficits in a student's fixed capacity to learn—not to missing prior knowledge. Therefore, when faced with a student who is not learning sufficiently, these people begin trying to solve the problem by considering ability deficits. That is a mistake. When a student has trouble learning, teachers should check to find out what the student does and does not know. To do this well, a teacher must understand that there are different types of knowledge.

In general, knowledge can take the form of facts, concepts, procedures, or metacognition (Anderson & Krathwohl, 2001). *Facts* and *concepts* can be thought of as "what" knowledge; they include the content that educators teach and students learn within any topical area (e.g., history, reading, art). *Procedures* can be thought of as "how" knowledge; it is the series of steps and rules for doing something. *Metacognition* is more like "why" or "when" knowledge; it includes self-awareness of learning and knowledge in relation to why the other types of knowledge are important or when they should be used, applied, or accessed.

Educational tasks should be thought of as amalgamations of facts, concepts, procedures, and metacognition. No task is purely factual, conceptual, or procedural. In addition, the information we teach does not become knowledge until it is incorporated into the student's cognitive repertoire or schema. The importance of using teaching to transform the *potential* information being taught into knowledge that a student can directly access and use is paramount. This issue is particularly salient given the extent to which *materials* often drive instruction.

In this book, when we refer to "curriculum," we are not referring to "materials." Most materials commonly found in classrooms contain lots of information that potentially may be useful for some students to learn depending on what the students already know and what they will be expected to do with the information. These same materials also contain information that, for some students, is already known or won't be useful without additional context or knowledge. It is the teacher's job to engage in a thoughtful selection process to identify the information that is most relevant, given the student's current level of performance.

Curriculum materials serve an important function in schools because they eliminate the need for teachers to "start from scratch" in deciding what to teach so that students can meet the grade-level standards. However, curriculum materials should be thought of as the parts list rather than the blueprint for designing instruction. Some of the "parts" contained in materials can be used right off the shelf. Other information contained in curriculum materials may need to be modified to make it accessible for a particular student.

Let's take a closer look at the types of knowledge.

Factual Knowledge

Factual knowledge is sometimes called rote or declarative knowledge (Marzano et al., 1988). Here are some examples of facts: "6 times 8 is 48," "James A. Garfield was the 20th president of the United States," and "the atomic weight of helium is 4.0026." Here is another fact, in case you are in need of motivation right now: the average salary for college graduates is about $1,250 a month higher than the average salary of high school graduates (U.S. Department of Education, National Center on Education Statistics, 2012). Facts are discrete bits of information that stand alone. For example, knowing that the capital of Indiana is Indianapolis does not lead one to know that the capital of Switzerland is Bern.

Facts are things a person can know without knowing how to figure them out or what they mean. Learning facts entails memorization, and instruction designed to teach facts must focus on moving the information from short-term memory to long-term memory through repeated rehearsal distributed over time (Simmons & Kame'enui, 1990). This is a different approach than used with conceptual knowledge.

Conceptual Knowledge

Concepts are a collection of defining characteristics shared by a set of objects, events, actions, or situations. The defining characteristics are the critical features of all members of the category that provide the basis for organizing the attributes of the concept and for distinguishing between examples and nonexamples of the concept. Conceptual knowledge permits a student to grasp the implications and underlying ideas associated with an idea as well as simplify the memorization of factual knowledge by organizing the bits of information into categories or classifications. For example, the concept of "square" may include the defining characteristics of "four equal sides" and "four interior right angles." Those relevant features help differentiate a square (example) from a circle (nonexample) by focusing on critical features (sides, angles) instead of nonessential ones (color, size).

Concepts are best taught through presentation of examples and nonexamples that illustrate the full range of the concept class. For example, to teach the concept "metal," a range of elements that qualify as metals would be presented as positive examples, whereas transition or metalloid elements might be presented as minimally different nonexamples. Some concepts are difficult to teach and learn because they are made complex by conditional or nested attributes (or the examples have membership in multiple categories).

Consider for example, the concept "boat" defined as "a small watercraft." Examples could include "canoe," "rowboat," "rowing shell," and "sailboat." However, larger craft often are referred to as "boats" too, so something as big as an automobile ferry or a tugboat seems to qualify as a "boat." If you were interested in finding out whether a particular student was lacking prior knowledge about boats, you might first need to specify what you mean by "boat." This idea seems somewhat confusing when thinking about noun concepts like "boat," and it becomes more difficult when the concept under consideration is "correct spelling," "two-step problem solving," or "appropriate talk."

Procedural Knowledge

Procedures are composed of a series of steps for actually performing a task and rules for when the procedure needs to be applied. Procedures are content specific and are sometimes conditional. For example, there are specific procedures for changing the tires of a vehicle. Those procedures differ for changing a bicycle's tire or changing a 747's tire. Often there is more than one way to do something correctly (and there are definitely many ways to do something incorrectly).

If two students with the same factual and conceptual knowledge follow different procedures, one may succeed at the task whereas the other might fail. For example, think about how you would solve this problem:

$$14(27 - x) = 56$$

First, you would divide both sides by 14. You'd get:

$$27 - x = 4$$

Next, you'd subtract 4 from both sides. You'd get:

$$23 - x = 0$$

Finally, you'd add x to both sides. You'd get:

$$23 = x$$

Here is the information you probably used to arrive at this solution.

1. This problem requires me to solve for the unknown.
2. If I isolate the unknown (x) on one side of the equation, I can solve for it.
3. If I do something to one side of the equation, I need to do it to the other side.
4. If I subtract a number from itself, I get 0.

Notice that the steps used for solving the problem involve a series of rules, and that nested within these rules are various concepts (things like "unknown" and "equation") and facts (such as "56 divided by 14 equals 4" and "$23 - 23 = 0$").

The procedural knowledge you employed informed you of *what* to do and *when* to do it. You might not have been consciously aware of all of the steps you followed to solve the problem if all of the component information is part of your background knowledge. However, if you were missing *any* of the key pieces of information, you might not have been able to solve the problem.

Metacognitive Knowledge

Metacognition is often described as "cognition about cognition" or "thinking about thinking." It involves an understanding and awareness of your own thinking in terms of general strategies for learning as well as self-assessment of how well one understands something.

As mentioned above, procedural knowledge is content specific and generally applies to a limited range of tasks. Strategies are more general and may be used across several content domains. Learning strategies are for remembering information and might be categorized into rehearsal strategies (repeated practice) and elaboration strategies (explanation or description) (Weinstein & Mayer, 1986). Organizational strategies such as outlining and note taking also fall into the category of general strategies that facilitate or enable learning.

The other aspect of metacognitive knowledge is awareness of one's own strengths and needs. This self-awareness is in relation to the degree of proficiency one has in applying procedures, the amount or content of facts and concepts within a content area, and proficiency with strategies. As educators, we can often fall into the trap of considering knowledge (and with it, curriculum and instruction) in isolation or as the product we deliver. When we examine the plethora of information we have at hand, we make determinations about a student's proficiency with certain skills by comparing his performance to a standard. We generally then design instruction to move the student from "not proficient" to "proficient." However, if the student believes that he is "proficient" or doesn't understand what "not proficient" means, it can be like trying to walk a sleeping dog—it is difficult even though the dog isn't trying to be noncompliant. Yet that is the attribution we might make if we don't check the student's understanding of his knowledge and skills (or look to see if the dog is asleep before pulling on the leash).

As an example, one of us was working with a student, Walter, who picked out some books for us to read and discuss. Looking at the little sticker that someone had put on the corner of the cover of the top book, Walter said, "Oh, I can't read that, it's a level P book.

I'm at level M." When asked what that meant, Walter explained that P was harder than M and that therefore, he did not have the skills to read that book. Of course, we had already worked with Walter and had other sources of information (his reading accuracy and fluency in relation to an empirically derived standard, lexile analysis of this and other texts) that indicated this book (and others at "level P") would be very appropriate for Walter because it would be challenging, but not too frustrating for us to read together. After looking at the actual text, explaining what we were doing and why we were doing it, and giving him our reasoning about why this would be a good book to use, Walter agreed that it would be suitable. In fact, Walter read the book nearly error-free, quite fluently, and comprehended what he read. Our knowledge of Walter's skills was based on different sources than Walter's self-knowledge, which turned out to be based on misconceptions of proficiency and what text leveling systems mean.

CONFRONT COMMON MISCONCEPTIONS THAT INFLUENCE TEACHING

The example of Walter shows how misconceptions can influence learning. Students aren't the only ones who can have misconceptions, however. Teachers' misconceptions about learning can have a disastrous impact on their effectiveness. There are many misconceptions that direct our focus to things that are not important or provide excuses for not focusing our efforts on certain students. In addition to focusing on alterable variables and keeping in mind that all students can learn, other commonly held misconceptions include those about task difficulty, learning styles, motivation, and practice.

Task Complexity Is Not the Same as Task Difficulty

Understanding the functional and conceptual role of prior knowledge is sometimes difficult because it has implications that seem counterintuitive. For example, consider the idea of task difficulty. To most of us, driving a car is no harder than fixing lunch, and reading this page is no harder than cleaning up after lunch. That is because we are adequately skilled to do all of these things. However, not everyone is. Tasks become difficult when we don't have adequate prior knowledge and skill to do them. Because we all have different prior knowledge, tasks that are hard for one person may be easy for another.

It is common to hear a student say something is "hard" (it may be accompanied by whining). For that student, experience with that task may *feel* hard because he doesn't have the necessary prior knowledge or experience to have mastered the skill or prerequisite skills to perform it. It should be less common to hear teachers say to students that something is hard, because what they usually mean is that it is either complex (involving many steps or a lot of prior knowledge) or is at the boundary of what the student knows and does not yet know.

Task difficulty does not reside in the task; it resides in the interaction of the task and the learner's prior knowledge. This means that the students with the fewest mastered skills have the hardest time in school. On the face of it, this seems pretty obvious. It is unfortunate, as has already been pointed out, that many people attribute learning difficulty to deficits in a student's fixed capacity to learn—not to missing prior knowledge. Therefore, when faced with a student who is not learning, they begin trying to solve the problem by considering ability deficits. That is a mistake. When a student has trouble learning, teachers should check to find out what the student does and does not know and then teach him what he does not yet know.

So what we usually mean when we talk about a task being hard is that it is complex or involves skills and knowledge that the student has not yet mastered. Describing a task as harder than another generally means that it is more complex—that it requires more prior knowledge. So what we say to a student who is concerned that a task is too hard is:

"You know how you're really good at [something he's good at]? You haven't always been. The more you've done it, the better you've gotten because now you know more about how to [same thing he's good at] than you used to. [Concerning task] is the same way; once you learn and practice it, it will *seem* easier than it does now."

Practice Isn't Everything

The notion that tasks get easier with practice comes from the belief that learning occurs gradually in the same way that muscles are built. Learning doesn't occur gradually, it occurs almost instantaneously when new information is linked to prior knowledge. Therefore, learning is best assisted through explanation or demonstration that builds connections between what is already known and what is about to be learned. *Proficiency* is what builds gradually. It is how well you use what you've learned. Therefore, improved proficiency requires a lot of practice (with ample feedback).

CBE MAXIM #4:

You can only practice what you already know!

Practice is appropriate at the right point in the instructional sequence and certainly valuable, but the student must already have learned something to practice it. He also needs the motivation to sustain the practice.

Motivation Should Be about Accomplishment More Than Completion

It is often thought that **motivation** can be developed by giving students "easy" things to do (yes, "ease" is the intersection of task requirements and student knowledge; we knew we couldn't slip that past you). Many people confuse the idea of successful completion of a task, even a task that does not require much attention or effort, with the idea of *accomplishing* a goal. However, motivation does not come with successful completion alone; it comes with the sense of control and **accomplishment** (Carbonneau, Vallerand, & Lafreniere, 2012). Motivation is promoted by the student's adaptive interpretation of *both* successes and failures. Such adaptive interpretations are themselves promoted by how teachers and parents respond to and *explain* the successes and failures in students' lives (Giangreco, Edelman, Luiselle, & MacFarland, 1997). Of interest, it is very hard for some teachers to accept that motivation is learned. To them, selective attention and memory may seem alterable, but motivation is a different story. This may be because some people associate motivation with "wanting to learn." In fact, there are many students who want to learn but fail because they have acquired maladaptive motivational strategies. There are probably just as many students with effective motivational strategies who learn easily despite limited interest in the topic.

Motivation is often equated with **perseverance.** The student who works on something the longest, particularly in the face of difficulty or negative feedback, seems the most motivated. Some students work harder in the face of difficulty, whereas others with equal skills give up.

Why?

Many researchers believe that some skilled students fail to persevere because they suffer from **learned helplessness**. According to motivation theory, learned helplessness is rooted in mistaken beliefs about success and failure. Students who have been taught that positive outcomes are the result of external factors like luck, easy assignments, or pampering teachers don't become motivated. Neither do students who believe success is the result of unalterable, internal factors like high intelligence (Dweck, 1986; Landfried, 1989; Schunk, 1996; Seligman, 1990).

How effectively a person works is determined in part by his beliefs about himself, his skills, and the assignments on which he is working. When a student believes that things he can't control cause failure, the onset of difficulty (i.e., increased effort needed to maintain performance) becomes a signal to quit working.

In contrast, a student who believes that success is related to things he can control (e.g., how much effort he puts into work) views the same difficulty as a cue to work harder. On reading comprehension assignments, a student who believes he is helpless will skip over a passage that is difficult to understand. On the other hand, a student who believes he has control over his own success, upon encountering a difficult passage, will slow his reading rate, reread the passage, or consult needed resources.

One maladaptive motivational pattern is that completing tasks or assignments is more important than learning. This is interesting because, whereas all teachers want students to feel successful, many teachers do not understand that students may define success in different ways. Dweck (1986) draws a distinction between *learning* and *performance* definitions of success. According to her theory, a student with a **learning orientation** believes that success comes with progress toward learning goals, and a student with a **performance orientation** believes success comes with completing work.

A learning orientation is adaptive because it allows students to find success in challenging work as long as they improve, even when they don't correctly complete it (Schunk, 1996). In contrast, the performance orientation may lead a student to develop techniques for finishing assignments regardless of learning (e.g., by turning them in with errors or copying from other students). This maladaptive motivational pattern may be fostered when teachers instruct students to "get this assignment done by recess," rather than instructing them to "use this assignment to learn new vocabulary skills."

Learning Preferences Exist; Learning Styles Don't

A different way of thinking that students have a fixed capacity for learning is that students have a fixed way of learning. In this learning-style view, learning problems are often conceptualized as the result of the student's "unique learning style." Many people also believe that these styles can be identified through testing and used to enhance individualized instruction. This second belief, that styles of learning can be accurately measured and then used as the basis for selecting how to teach, seems to cause problems.

To remedy learning problems, advocates of learning-styles instruction (LSI) recommend testing students to map out their cognitive and/or perceptual styles so that instructional techniques, which are thought to complement those preferences, can be selected (Carbo, 1992; Chan, 1996; Tobias, 1994). However, for decades LSI has been refuted (Arter & Jenkins, 1979; Glass, 1983; Kavale, 1981; Lakin, 1983; Pashler, McDaniel, Rohrer, & Bjork, 2008; Snider, 1992; Ulman & Rosenberg, 1986; Waugh, 1975).

The scientific fact is that there is very little truth to the myth of *learning styles*. However, this is another case of using the same term to mean different things (we're good at that in education). What most people mean when they talk about learning styles is actually *learning preferences*. Some students prefer certain methods of instructional delivery because it aligns with their prior knowledge, proficiency with procedures, and their metacognitive knowledge including both general strategies and self-awareness.

When educators use LSI (i.e., test for an individual's fixed strengths and weaknesses and use the results to make long-range predictions about how they should be taught) they are making a mistake. However, LSI shouldn't be confused with selecting different objectives for students at different skill levels or with assuming that some interventions are more effective than others. Those beliefs are accurate.

USE VARIED TEACHING APPROACHES

When talking about instruction, it is necessary to use terms like *type, approach, program, method, style, orientation*, and even *philosophy*. These are used to differentiate among various ways of teaching. There seems to be an almost endless debate about the relative superiority of these different ways to teach. One reason these debates are so bewildering is that it is often impossible to tell whether the contestants are arguing about *what* should be taught (i.e., curriculum) or about *how* it should be taught (i.e., instruction). Although it is unlikely that this section is going to put these quarrels to rest, it is important to mention them to make the processes and procedures in this book easier to understand.

Often the debate comes down to two methods, the main contestants being the *generative* approach and the *supplantive* approach (lest any combatant in the instruction wars claim bias, we shall present them alphabetically). The generative approach is often referred to as "constructivist" or "inquiry based," and the supplantive approach is often referred to as "behaviorist" or "direct instruction." The two approaches are contrasted in Table 2.2. The problem with comparisons like these is that they are so binary that they prohibit com-

TABLE 2.2. A Comparison of Teaching Approaches

Attribute	Generative approach	Supplantive approach
Buzzwords used by proponents	Constructivist, developmental, holistic, authentic	Behaviorist, direct instruction, mastery learning, task analytic
What opponents call it	Fuzzy, fluffy, postmodern	Reductionist, drill-and-kill, inauthentic
Underlying beliefs about what is taught	1. Students construct their own understandings. 2. When learning is contextualized, students will identify when they are ready to learn.	The skills that students need to learn can be derived from an analysis of the social demands placed on them.
Underlying beliefs about how learning occurs	1. Learning is socially constructed; students link new information to prior knowledge when provided opportunities to observe or experience. 2. Learning is developmental and occurs much the same way early language is acquired.	1. Learning can be induced through instruction that builds explicit links between new information and prior knowledge. 2. When learning does not occur, it can be facilitated by building it from the "bottom up" through teaching of prerequisite skills.
Underlying beliefs about how to teach	Teachers take a "hands-off" approach and seek to provide a meaningful context in which learning will occur naturally.	Teachers take a "hands-on" approach by structuring lessons and providing explicit direction.
Common error made by proponents	1. Creating interesting classroom activities, but failing to link these to learning outcomes. 2. Too much emphasis on larger ideas, not enough on components.	1. By focusing on specific learning outcomes, they may fail to attend to other equally important interests and topics. 2. Too much emphasis on components, not enough on the larger ideas.

promise (sounds political, doesn't it?), so they always misrepresent someone and leave something out. Besides, the two approaches frequently seem to differ more in explanation than in practice. For example, many generative methods include explicit directions for students who have failed to discover needed information, and many supplantive methods involve purposefully planning portions of the day for students to explore and experiment with their own learning.

Proponents from both "camps" have been guilty of heated and at times silly rhetoric during the past two decades. It is unfortunate that much of the so-called "debate" has been philosophical rather than scientific. However, the crux of the difference between the two approaches comes down to two issues: (1) the role of the teacher in the teaching and learning process and (2) the timing for presentation of information.

With a supplantive approach, the teacher attempts to promote learning by providing explicit directions and explanations regarding how to do a task. The teacher assumes primary responsibility for linking new information with the student's prior knowledge and, ultimately, what the student learns. As a consequence, with a supplantive approach information usually is presented in an ordered sequence in which component subskills are taught directly as a foundation for later tasks. In this respect, a supplantive approach to instruction is highly *teacher directed.*

With a generative approach, the teacher functions as a facilitator who takes a less central role in a learning process that is *student directed* (Engle, 2006). The teacher provides opportunities for the student to make his own linkages to prior knowledge and to devise his own strategies for work. Generative instruction is "constructivist" because much of its emphasis is on helping students construct their own educational goals and experiences as well as the knowledge that results. With this approach, information usually is presented on a schedule determined by student interests and goals. With generative instruction, subskills may not be taught explicitly. Prerequisites for more complex information are expected to be learned as a consequence of the larger understandings students would be guided to construct.

With the generative approach to instruction, learning is assumed to be socially constructed out of the interaction between the student's innate tendencies and predisposition (following the student's own timeline) and the social context in which the student lives (Stone, 1996). But advocates of the generative approach sometimes take a restrictive view of social context. Often, they do not seem to view teachers and classrooms as part of the social context. Therefore, they see intentional instruction by teachers (or parents for that matter) as "unnatural" and "meaningless." However, as Stone (1996) puts it, "Developmentalism . . . fails to recognize the extent to which valued social, emotional, and cognitive attributes may be induced and sustained (not merely facilitated) by the purposeful actions of teachers and parents" (p. 20). A critique of the generative position on development is that it is condescending to teachers because it diminishes their role in student learning as well as the importance of their teaching skills. It is then argued that purely generative approaches relinquish the teacher's responsibility for teaching by turning instructional decision making over to the student.

Supplantive approaches have also been accused of being condescending to teachers to the extent that instruction may seem formulaic or contrived. For example, the DISTAR reading materials, originally developed for use by untrained paraprofessionals working in the early Head Start programs, were based on a direct instruction approach (Adams & Engelmann, 1996; Barbash, 2012). These materials were designed to be "teacher proof," with scripted lessons and procedures that untrained implementers were expected to follow verbatim. For many, these so-called teacher-proof materials have come to epitomize a direct approach to instruction. This perception is inaccurate and unfortunate, because it perpetuates the confusion of curriculum materials with instructional approach. Clearly, a teacher turning all responsibility for decision making over to the curriculum materials relinquishes the same amount of responsibility for teaching as one who turns it all over to students to direct.

Effective Teaching

Early research on teaching focused almost exclusively on the personal characteristics of teachers. These characteristics included things like their form of dress, gender, sense of humor, race, and voice. The assumption driving this research was that certain types of people make good teachers. The results were kind of silly and easier to understand in terms of public relations than instruction. In addition, because the things being studied were almost impossible to alter, the research results were nearly useless to teacher trainers (Bloom, 1980).

Beginning in the mid-1970s, research on teaching changed dramatically as it shifted from an emphasis on the personal characteristics of teachers to the quality of their teaching. Using simple methods of observation and testing, researchers began to map out relations between certain teacher actions and student learning. This research identified sets of teacher actions that tend to promote student learning and have come to be called "effective teaching" (Good & Brophy, 2008; Marzano, Pickering, & Pollack, 2004). Effective teaching includes many specific components, but in general includes: (1) clear learning targets, (2) high academic engaged time, (3) formative assessment and progress monitoring, and (4) instructional variety (Borich, 2011).

Despite the Insert-Content-Area-Here Wars, what has been known for some time about effective teaching is that the instructional methods used must be varied according to the type of information being learned and the needs of the student. Effective instruction, by definition, must include both teacher-directed and student-directed components (Connor, Morrison, Fishman, Schatschneider, & Underwood, 2007). Sometimes scripting will be necessary and other times not.

The real issue is never *whether* to use an approach but *when* (Connor et al., 2007; Gersten & Dimino, 1993; Smith, 1992; Stahl & Kuhn, 1995).

Teaching Students Who Are Experiencing Learning Problems

In teaching, as with all things in life, there is a time and a place for everything. The question is "When should a generative approach be used and when should a supplantive approach be used?" Because of this idea, the generative and supplantive methods can never be in strict opposition. Instead, a teacher must be prepared to use the salient features of different instructional techniques. A teacher who only knows how to use a generative approach is as poorly equipped to meet the needs of her students as a teacher who only knows how to use a supplantive approach.

Students experiencing learning difficulty may not be sufficiently knowledgeable about the context to see the linkages that would make a generative approach meaningful. For example, whereas everyone would agree that letter sounds are ideally learned within the context of words, some students may have such limited knowledge of the concepts of print and sound that the presentation of multiple letters would simply confuse them. To address this problem, a supplantive approach would isolate initial sounds and teach them out of the context of words. The teacher may compensate for the resulting loss in contextual meaning by producing a temporary context of verbal praise, or even tangible rewards, to keep the student motivated and to make the lesson meaningful (Dev, 1997; Geary, 1995).

Isolating salient features and introducing rewards that the student already recognizes should not be considered artificial and at odds with the developmental philosophy because these steps of isolation and introducing known rewards are always meant to be temporary. The goal should always be to combine isolated skills and remove introduced rewards as soon as the student has sufficient skills to work with the context without the additional support.

Because this book is about decision making in order to solve a learning problem, much of the emphasis is on teacher-directed instruction. However, it is the responsibility of a skilled teacher to make an informed, reasoned decision about which instructional approach is appropriate for a particular skill for a particular student at a particular time. Some guidelines for deciding which approach (generative or supplantive) may be best for a particular situation are shown in Table 2.3. Many of the descriptors in that exhibit are explained elsewhere in this book.

TABLE 2.3. Guidelines for Selecting an Instructional Approach

	Select a generative approach when . . .	Select a supplantive approach when . . .
The student	• Has considerable prior knowledge of the task.	• Has little prior knowledge of the task.
	• Has adaptive motivational patterns.	• Has maladaptive motivational patterns.
	• Experiences consistent success on the task.	• Experiences repeated failure on the task.
The task	• Is well defined.	• Is poorly defined.
	• Can be completed using a general strategy.	• Requires use of a task-specific procedure.
	• Is complete or comprehensive.	• Is pivotal to the learning of subsequent tasks.
	• Is to understand, but not necessarily apply, what is learned.	• Must be used with a high level of proficiency.
		• Has missing information.
The setting	• Allows plenty of time to accomplish outcomes.	• Time allowed to accomplish outcomes is limited.
	• Places priority on experiences and activities.	• Places priority on task mastery.

KEEP AN OPEN AND POSITIVE OUTLOOK

What we as educators believe about learning affects the way we teach (Ball & Cohen, 1996; Shulman, 1986). In addition, what we think about the individual learning characteristics of our students also influences our interactions with those students in class (Lipman, 1997). This has been shown with both student evaluation (Cadwell & Jenkins, 1986; Hemingway, Hemingway, Hutchinson, & Kuhns, 1987) and teacher expectation in general (Teddlie et al., 1989).

There actually have been a lot of changes in the field of learning theory over the past 30 years. This is especially true in relation to learning problems. As such, we can expect that not all teachers will share a common view of learning. Yet the decision-making process is typically shaped by what we know and what we value. The decisions we make hinge as much on our own knowledge about learning as they do on observations of and attitude toward individual students.

A strong and consistent finding in the research literature is that when a teacher holds high expectations for a student, that student is much more likely to learn (Figlio & Lucas, 2004). It also means that when teachers have low expectations and write off a student, that student won't learn. Sometimes this happens because we overemphasize something that puts the student at risk for learning problems or assume it actually causes learning problems. Other times, it happens because we have worked with the student for so long and so hard without seeing the results we wanted that we become frustrated. It becomes so much more rewarding to switch our attention and energy elsewhere. And unfortunately, sometimes it happens because the expectation that learning will occur is blocked by bias introduced through gossip ("he's just like his brother"), disability labels, and even racial/ethnic or gender stereotypes.

When we write off students, the effort we put into teaching and solving the learning problems of the written-off student drops and we divert it elsewhere. When working with students who are experiencing learning problems, it is often difficult to remember the idealism of the first day on the job. This can be true even when there are reminders.

For example, in the entryway of a school that one of us visited, there was a plaque that read "*At our school we believe all students can learn.*" However, in a meeting that day, many of the teachers seemed to be spending time trying to convince the visitor that a student named Rocco *couldn't* learn. The talk about this student was so negative and the thinking of the teachers was so closed that nothing recommended to help Rocco even seemed to be considered. Rocco had been written off. In a desperate effort to get Rocco back into the picture, we made a sign that said "*except* Rocco" and taped it under the entryway plaque where every visiting parent and civic leader would see it. No one seemed amused by this juxtaposition of school philosophy and teacher expectation (except maybe Rocco), and none of the staff really wanted to agree with a sign that read "*At our school we believe all students can learn—except Rocco.*"

Every teacher we have worked with *wants* to help all children succeed; however, we have worked with many teachers who do not *believe* all children can succeed. Without that belief, even the strongest desire to help children succeed will fail because of the undermining effect that will have on our decision making, our judgment, and the instruction we provide.

CHAPTER SUMMARY

This chapter has been about some of the key concepts to implementing CBE. Some might be helpful as a type of mission statement (keep an open and positive outlook), others can enhance (e.g., focus on alterable variables) or derail (e.g., the misconceptions) our attempts at doing our best to help our students learn. And others provide a foundation for everything else we discuss in this book—types of knowledge, use varied teaching approaches. Just as it is important to monitor the fidelity of the instruction we provide, it is important to consider fidelity of the methods of decision making we use. From time to time, the information contained in this chapter can be helpful as a sort of "daily CBE affirmation" to reset your thinking if you find that the details of the process get complex or difficult or you find that your implementation of the CBE process does not produce the desired results.

CHAPTER 3

Overview of the CBE Process of Inquiry

In the preceding chapters, we discussed a great deal of information about evaluation, measurement, curriculum, the nature of learning problems, and so on—clarifying the background information important to using CBE. This chapter presents a critical shift in the balance of this book. The rest of the book will not provide as much in the way of rationale and background. From here on out, we assume you are up to speed on *why* to use CBE and core foundations for CBE, so we will primarily explain *how to do* CBE.

THE CBE PROCESS OF INQUIRY

Figure 3.1 is a visual representation of the CBE process. It can be considered a *heuristic overlay*—that is, it is a series of steps that are experience based in order to guide the user through the process of making educational decisions for the purpose of instructional planning, implementation, and evaluation. It is an overlay in that the process can be applied to any content area. No matter the differences in specific details when making instructional decisions about reading comprehension for a 10th-grade student or science for a first grader (and there should be many differences), the general process of inquiry should remain consistent. There are certain actions that need to take place and certain questions that must be answered. If the process does not produce the desired outcomes, there are certain ordered steps one should take to identify where the process broke down or went awry.

The CBE process is composed of 3 phases, 12 actions, 3 questions, and 1 five-step troubleshooting system. The phases are the broad components of the process that roughly align with the components of any problem solving system: Phase 1 is about identifying and

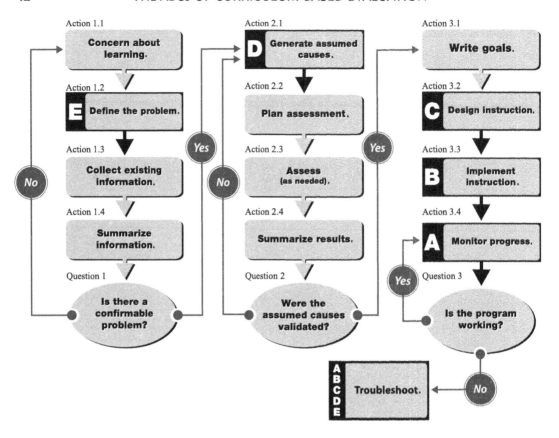

FIGURE 3.1. The CBE process of inquiry.

validating the presence of a problem; Phase 2 is about analyzing the problem; and Phase 3 is about solving the problem. Although presented visually as linear, in practice they will often be iterative—requiring you to cycle through the actions a few times, possibly returning to the beginning action of the phase and clarifying performance of an action before moving on to answer the question that allows one to move to the next phase. While the actions are designed to occur in a generally consistent order, there is no set amount of time one should spend on each action or question. Nor, we would argue, should there be. The amount of time to spend is always as much as you need to complete that action appropriately or to answer the question accurately with assurance. If you can do that quickly without sacrificing accuracy or specificity, great.

The actions are the more specific sets of tasks that are completed within each phase. You probably noticed (good for you!) that each action box starts with an action word. While the fundamental rationale for CBE is about educator *thinking*, ultimately the outcomes we effect with our students is about educator *doing*. Just because we thought about little Hubert being able to read better, it doesn't equate to him reading better—at least not due to our help. If you are looking for a way to evaluate your own performance through the use of the CBE process (and you should be), you can use those action words for each step as a sort of check. For example, Action 1.3 is "Collect existing information." You can ask yourself (1) if you collected information, and (2) if that information was most or all of what was already existing and relevant. If you feel confident answering both questions with a "yes," then you should feel confident moving on to the next step.

Speaking of questions, the questions in the CBE process act as a sort of gate from one phase to the next. Similar to checking how you did on each step by informally asking whether you performed the action in the step, the formal questions are ones that you have to be able to answer in order to move on to another phase. We consider them the "good for the goose, good for the gander" part of the process. If we are expected to formatively evaluate the student's performance, why shouldn't we formatively evaluate our own?

CAUTION!

An important point to remember is that if you skip a step or do not complete it sufficiently (or accurately), you will be less likely to answer the question positively and will be sent back to repeating the phase (not as punishment, but as corrective feedback).

Consider the case of Edsel Elementary. Edsel Elementary has a Data Team system where all the teachers of a grade level meet once a month to discuss student performance and collaborate on planning interventions and instruction. They use CBE as the framework for their decision making, but have decided that they could save time by not explicitly considering each action and question. They typically go directly from confirming the problem, which is done by examining the student's performance on the universal screening instruments, to designing an intervention based on that performance (ignoring Phase 2: Summative Decision Making, where the actual missing prerequisite skills or knowledge would be identified).

Ms. Smedley, who is very familiar with CBE, is new to Edsel Elementary. She is concerned by this skipping of Phase 2. Midway through the school year, she expresses her concern, and is given the explanation that it saves the team time to skip Phase 2 so that they can have more time to provide instruction. Although she cannot argue with the logic, she flips back through her notes from the Data Team meetings that year and notices that of the 16 students who have been discussed, 10 were discussed multiple times because the intervention as designed was not working. Despite the interventions being implemented appropriately (i.e., with high fidelity), the students were not improving in their performance.

What the team at Edsel Elementary was doing was noting poor performance in a broad area (reading or math) and picking an intervention that was available. Because they were skipping Phase 2, they were missing the consideration of whether the intervention addressed the problem because they had not verified the problem. Although every student demonstrated poor performance in reading or math, not all of their problems were due to that student having not mastered certain skills. Ms. Smedley argued that saving about 15 minutes in the meeting and another 15–20 minutes of assessment time to verify assumed causes, was offset by the additional 30 minutes of discussion that resulted for 10 of the 16 students. This is in addition to at least a month of intervention time that could have been provided to each student. Without explicitly evaluating what they did and confirming the decisions they made, the team worked to address the same problem multiple times.

Problems encountered like those at Edsel Elementary have the unintended consequence of using up more time you would have had for instruction in the process of assessment and decision making. Assessment and decision making are clearly important, but at the end of the day it is teaching that is most likely to increase student learning. Therefore, you want to spend the least amount of time possible on assessment and decision making that is required to give you the information you need to make the most accurate decisions. Being aware of the amount of information needed for each action and being planful in our collection and judgment of that information lets us be as efficient as possible while still increasing the probability of making good decisions.

CBE MAXIM #5:

When in doubt, teach!

The rest of this chapter will walk you through the CBE process of inquiry in general terms—what each phase is for, what each action should lead you to do, and why we ask each question. Although the descriptions involve specific references to the performance of "the student," it is important to remember that the process can be just as useful for groups of students, classrooms, or grade levels. We address these applications in Chapter 4 on Phase 1: Fact Finding.

PHASE 1: FACT FINDING

Phase 1 involves the broad process of problem identification and validation—determining whether there is a problem that we can confirm by collecting and synthesizing the information that is already known. In general, this phase is about two things. First, fact finding is about determining the level at which the problem resides. Although concerns are often expressed about an individual student's performance, the best solution is not necessarily to intervene with only that student. It can be more efficient to intervene with a small group, whole class, or even whole grade level. Second, fact finding is about determining how the student (or group of students) is currently performing, how the student should be performing, and whether the difference between the two is meaningful.

Action 1.1: Concern about Learning

Concerns about learning come from many sources: the classroom teacher might notice that a student does not seem to be "getting it," parents might contact the school because their child seems to lack an understanding of how to complete his homework, universal screening data may identify a student as performing well below criterion in multiple areas. No matter where a concern about learning comes from, it should be taken seriously and examined. Not all concerns will be confirmed (at least as they were originally expressed), but just receiving an expression of concern should suggest that somewhere there is a discrepancy between what someone expects and how the student is performing, or how someone perceives that student to be performing.

Action 1.2: Define the Problem

Once the concern about learning has been brought to your attention, it is important to begin to narrow down exactly what the concern is. While a statement such as "Hubert has trouble reading" is often enough to determine there is a concern about learning (Action 1.1), it is not specific enough to guide the collection of data in order to validate the presence of a problem that needs remediation. This step is about making that concern into a statement or series of questions that can be used as the foundation for the rest of the CBE process. While all the actions are important, this represents a critical juncture: if the problem is not adequately defined, all the decisions and actions coming after will be misaligned. This is one of the most common errors of the CBE process that we see.

Action 1.3: Collect Existing Information

Much of the data needed for Phase 1 will already be collected, so the important part is to bring them all together and put them into a form that assists in summarizing and decision making. Relevant data can be direct measures of the area of concern (e.g., reading comprehension) or they can involve ruling out other potential areas that might lead to that difficulty (e.g., expressive and receptive language). An important consideration in this action is to ensure you collect information that is not just focused on the individual student, but can be aggregated across students (groups, classes, grade levels) to make decisions about the instruction as it is delivered, the curriculum as designed and enacted, as well as other setting-related characteristics that might affect learning. If the data collected are not sufficient to make decisions about sources of the problem other than learner characteristics, you will be led to make assumptions and reach conclusions that will not be supported later in the process. That would take up more valuable time than the extra effort of collecting those data now. Another consideration is that the data sources have appropriate technical adequacy. While some sources without reliability and validity evidence can be valuable (e.g., health history, review of prior grades, description of interventions tried), those that involve direct measures of student performance or those that involve whole-class or grade performance, must meet certain standards.

Action 1.4: Summarize Information

The collection of relevant data generally involves multiple sources, different types of data, and judgments using varying standards. Especially if conducting the CBE process as a team, some members will place greater emphasis on some pieces of information than others—and these emphases will probably not be consistent across members. Care should be taken to ensure that judgments were made about not just the individual student, but also groups, the class as a whole, the grade level, instruction, the curriculum, and setting characteristics. This summary should align with the definition of the problem in order to be able to answer Question 1, not just in confirming its presence but also in ruling out other potential problems that would need different solutions.

Question 1: Is There a Confirmable Problem?

This is the first major gate of decision making. If there is not a clearly identifiable problem that can be agreed on, it presents a challenge. When Question 1 cannot be answered affirmatively, or when there is disagreement about the answer, it is a time to reflect on the conduct of the actions in Phase 1. If a clear mistake in conduct or decision making can be identified, a clear solution probably exists. If not, it is necessary to go back through Phase 1 again (reviewing what was done and what was decided) in order to be able to answer Question 1 affirmatively. When it can be answered affirmatively and in agreement by all those involved, you should move directly to Phase 2: Summative Decision Making.

PHASE 2: SUMMATIVE DECISION MAKING

Phase 2 involves the process of problem analysis—determining what in the process of learning is breaking down and keeping the student from learning the material we want him/her to learn. In general, this phase is about working as an educational detective or scientist to develop hypotheses and test them in order to determine how best to intervene.

Action 2.1: Generate Assumed Causes

This is one of the most important steps in the CBE process, and in any problem-solving process, because it is one of the points when the best thinking has to be done. The things we think about here determine our next course of action. They can lead it to be quite efficient and fruitful or cumbersome and a waste of time. Based on the information collected and synthesized in Phase 1, hypotheses are developed about which aspects of the setting, curriculum, instruction, or learner might be altered in order to facilitate learning. These assumed causes (assumed because at this point we have not validated them yet, so we don't really know whether they are true causes) need to be explicitly stated about observable and measureable characteristics of learning. If they are not observable and measureable, the rest of the actions of Phase 2 become more difficult, decreasing the likelihood that we can answer Question 2 affirmatively.

Action 2.2: Plan Assessment

Before collecting additional information (remember, we want to be planful because assessing takes time we could use to teach), we want to know what information we need to collect.

This involves turning the assumed causes generated in Action 2.1 into questions. Once we know the questions, it becomes a lot easier to determine how best to answer them. The assessment plan is our guide for answering those questions. The assessment plan should address relevant information that aligns directly with the questions we need to answer. Some of the information is already known and corroborated from multiple sources; some of the information is known, but needs corroboration; and some of the information is unknown. These determinations also help guide the plan for assessment.

Action 2.3: Assess (as Needed)

Being planful in Actions 1.3 and 1.4 allows for a clear organization of what information is known. Being planful in Action 2.2 allows for a clear organization of what *relevant* information is unknown. Not all of the information we collected in Action 1.3 will end up being useful to generating and validating assumed causes. A key task is to determine *which* pieces of information are relevant for the task at hand. If information relevant to answering the questions generated from the assumed causes is already known, then there is probably no need to conduct additional assessment. If the information has come from a single source, is not very reliable, or was collected with questionable fidelity, then it is important to corroborate that information. The greater the stake of the decision, the more information must be collected.

Action 2.4: Summarize Results

In Action 1.4 we summarized all the information we had available in order to confirm the problem. In this step, the results of the assessment related to the assumed causes are used to answer the evaluation questions generated. As needed, the answers to the questions should be incorporated into the previously known information. This will help to provide the foundation for the next phase. However, the most important focus of this action is to make sure that the information collected is relevant and aligned enough to answer the questions we know we need to answer.

Question 2: Were the Assumed Causes Verified?

This is the second major gate of decision making. If the assumed causes were not verified, something went awry in the process. In this case, we need to go back to Action 2.1 and reconsider the assumed causes we generated. Why didn't we verify them? Maybe new information has come to light that changes our assumptions. For example, maybe we assumed that a student had difficulty with math story problems because he had difficulty with reading comprehension, but we assessed his reading comprehension and it is just fine. We would need to examine the information we summarized in Action 1.4 to generate and verify a different assumed cause.

PHASE 3: FORMATIVE DECISION MAKING

Phase 3 involves problem solution. This is the part that educators are often the most comfortable with because it is why you went into teaching in the first place—to help students, particularly those who are having difficulty. It is about providing the instruction or intervention the student needs in order to make sufficient educational progress and evaluating how that instruction or intervention is working. However, it is common for educators to go directly to trying solutions when a lot of time could be saved by being planful in selecting and developing those solutions.

Action 3.1: Write Goals

This is probably one of the most overlooked steps in any process of designing and providing instruction. Too often in our efforts to solve a problem we overlook having a strong understanding of the current state of things and a clear expectation of where we are headed. In teaching, this is a statement of the student's present level of performance—a statement of what the student can do proficiently and how he performs in the areas where he has difficulty. It should be the foundation of any goal. The goal is the target for performance or the criterion for how we will determine whether the instruction was successful. These are important steps in being planful.

Action 3.2: Design Instruction

Obviously, before we start teaching we need to plan what we will teach and how we will teach it. Selecting evidence-based strategies that have been validated for the specific needs of the student is a crucial component of CBE. Even with a strategy or program with good evidence to support its use, there are a lot of other considerations in terms of intensity, duration, grouping, and other scheduling concerns. Pulling a program off the shelf and using it without consideration for the specific student's needs can lead to problems if it doesn't lead to the improvements we expected.

Action 3.3: Implement Instruction

This is why we got into teaching, isn't it? To teach! Do your thing, but make sure to have a method of checking the fidelity of implementation. The best-designed instruction or intervention will not lead to improvements if it is not implemented correctly.

Action 3.4: Monitor Progress

Rather than waiting until the end of our prespecified time of instruction or intervention and then giving the student a task to complete in order to judge his performance, it is important to monitor progress consistently while we are implementing the instruction/intervention. Good assessment for making decisions about progress relies on standardized tools that have been demonstrated to have good reliability and validity as well as a stability in the forms or uses of the tool (sometimes referred to as alternate forms). This provides a consistent metric against which to compare the student's performance so that if he is not making adequate progress we know as soon as possible. And this helps us answer the question at the end of Phase 3.

Question 3: Is the Program Working?

There are a lot of ways to collect information to answer this question. If we were planful ahead of time, we already know how we will answer this question and we will have collected all of the data that we need to do so. To answer this question is merely to compare the information we have collected to the standard we set beforehand. If the student's performance is at or above the standard, then we congratulate him, celebrate the success, and move on to the next challenge. If the student's performance is below the standard, then we need to step back, appraise the information we have, and troubleshoot the CBE process to determine what we need to do differently. We keep doing this until the answer to Question 3 is a resounding "Yes!"

TROUBLESHOOT

If we have gone through the entire CBE process and the student has not met the objectives (i.e., we asked Question 3 and answered "no"), it means something in the process did not work as effectively or as efficiently as we planned. Rather than throwing up our hands in frustration (which might be the first impulse), this is the time to apply our problem-solving prowess to our application of the CBE process by essentially retracing our steps to determine where our implementation and the student's performance went off track. Rather than jumping back to the beginning and repeating the entire process, which is not very efficient, we can work backward from where we are. Also, rather than revisiting every single step, there are five steps that are most likely the ones where the process may have gone awry. These are the five CBE troubleshooting checkpoints.

Checkpoint A

The first step to double-check is that of monitoring progress. We need to make sure that the tool we selected to monitor student progress was implemented with fidelity, because changes in administration that differ from standardization can affect student performance. If the measure was implemented correctly, we need to reconsider whether it was the best measure to monitor progress and evaluate the effectiveness of the instruction/intervention. If we determine it was the best measure to use of the target skill or predictor, then we need to determine whether we selected the most appropriate skill to measure to monitor progress. If our troubleshooting of Action 3.4 does not turn up an area of concern to address, then we move on to Checkpoint B.

Checkpoint B

The next troubleshooting step is to check Action 3.3, our implementation of the instruction/intervention. Just like with the administration of progress monitoring tools, we need to ensure that our instruction/intervention was implemented as it was designed and validated to be implemented. If we were planful and have these data from observations and self-checks, troubleshooting is easier because we already have the information to review. If the instruction/intervention was implemented accurately, then we move on to Checkpoint C.

Checkpoint C

The next step in troubleshooting is to check Action 3.2, the design of the instruction/intervention implemented. We need to analyze how it might not have been intensive enough to elicit the learning we expected. There are a lot of characteristics of instruction and intervention that can be altered to make it more or less intensive—either intentionally or not. We also need to examine whether the instruction/intervention was sufficiently aligned with the student's need. The best-designed program will not be successful if it is not aligned with the student's need. If the instruction/intervention was designed well, then we move on to Checkpoint D.

Checkpoint D

The next step in troubleshooting is to check Action 2.1, the assumed causes we generated as hypotheses for the source of the student's difficulty. If the instruction/intervention was designed, implemented, and monitored properly, the stumbling block might be that we have designed a system to address the wrong need. It is possible that the decision about assumed causes was not accurate or complete, but it is also possible that this need that we are addressing is not the most pressing instructional need for the student. If the student is missing a prerequisite or enabling skill, it might be blocking learning the target skill. If the assumed causes were generated and validated, then we move on to Checkpoint E.

Checkpoint E

Action 1.2: Define the Problem, is the final stop of troubleshooting. If we have come all the way back to this point without finding a sufficient solution, something has gone quite awry in the CBE process. Although it is discouraging, these things do happen—sometimes new information comes to light that our old assumptions and hypotheses did not take into account. Sometimes we learn things through design and implementation of instruction/intervention that we could not have known beforehand, such as how a student will respond to different aspects of the program or how it will be practically implemented. When we arrive back at this position, it is important to step back and be able to critically evaluate every decision and piece of information, if necessary. Anyone who has ever critiqued their own work knows how difficult that can be. For this reason, it would be good to include a new individual or two into the process to give you a "new set of eyes," so to speak. The difficulty might not be in the information or implementation, but in the perspective offered on what the problem is and how to address it.

THE REST OF THIS BOOK

The rest of the book will be a walk-through of the phases of the CBE process. Specifics about each action will be provided as well as relevant forms (or guidelines for forms) that might be helpful as you implement the process.

CHAPTER 4

CBE Process Phase 1
Fact Finding

As we mentioned in Chapter 1, we consider the process of making decisions, and then implementing the actions involved in those decisions, as one of the most important functions in education. Educators are constantly making decisions. Many of these are ones that we have to make on the spur of the moment to address an immediate need; others are ones we can be more deliberate about. Clearly, the need to decide whether to take the scissors away from a student who is about to throw them across the room is not a decision for which we need to collect additional information (what's his motivation?). When working individually with a student and he says "I don't understand the directions," the immediate decision is to repeat them, possibly with additional clarification or a demonstration. While it is clearly an instructional decision (or a decision with instructional implications or consequences), it is not a decision with high stakes associated with the result. Use of a process of evaluation as systematic as CBE should be reserved for purposes that have high stakes and cannot be sufficiently resolved via simple decision making.

CBE MAXIM #6:

The higher the stakes of the decision, the greater the need for certainty!

THE PURPOSE OF PHASE 1: FACT FINDING

If you've ever watched a detective movie, a law or medical drama on television, or a congressional investigation, you've seen illustrations of the importance of fact finding. In any field, when making a decision, it is important to gather and summarize the facts of "what is

52

already known" before moving on to the process of collecting new information. To skip fact finding is to risk using some of our precious time redoing something to collect information we already had at our disposal. It would be like preparing for a vacation by taking your car to get the oil changed and gas tank filled, only to find that the oil was brand-new and the tank full. That time spent duplicating activities could have been put to good use packing or getting on the road a little early.

The majority of medical errors are flaws in thinking rather than technical or implementation flaws (Groopman, 2007). Through ample use of checklists and structured decision-making models, medical procedures are generally implemented with high fidelity. However, if a physician missed a presenting symptom or did not rule out alternate hypotheses, then the treatment would not be aligned with the actual need of the patient, and the result would not be the desired one. A classic example of this is the overuse of antibiotics. Antibiotics can be effective for treating bacterial infections (although different antibiotics have different levels of efficacy, particularly for different bacterial strains), but they are useless for viral infections. There are certainly tests to help determine whether the source of a sinus infection is viral or bacterial. However, because the tests are costly and take time to produce results, many physicians used to forgo those tests, assume a bacterial infection, and prescribe antibiotics. Not only would the antibiotics be ineffective for helping overcome viral infections, but the unintended consequence is that we have an increasing number of bacteria strains resistant to what were once effective medications.

In education, our needs are obviously a little different. We are unlikely to develop a resistant strain of reading problem because of overuse of an instructional strategy for misaligned purposes. However, our time and resources are at a premium. We need to be efficient in our determinations of what is needed and how to provide it. Similar "thinking errors" as experienced in medicine are also experienced in education (refer back to the threats to good judgment in Chapter 2). Use of a structured decision-making framework such as CBE can help, but ultimately the quality of the outcomes depends on the quality of the thinking that goes into the process. That process always starts with a concern about learning and works through a series of actions until we can confirm the presence of a problem or not (see Figure 4.1).

ACTION 1.1: CONCERN ABOUT LEARNING

Learning is clearly at the heart of what we expect from education in any form. It is also generally a strong social value in that we strive to develop "lifelong learners" of our students. But our students aren't the only learners in our schools. As educators, we are constantly in a position to learn new things and incorporate them into our practice. Invariably, what we learn today is influenced by what we have learned before. Often this is a good thing (e.g., learning to read fluently because we have a good grasp of the alphabetic principle and have strong phonemic awareness skills); but sometimes it can be problematic. While prior knowledge is a good facilitator of learning and often one of the stronger predictors of future performance, occasionally prior knowledge can be a barrier to learning.

Action 1.1

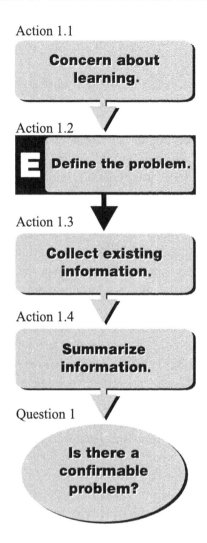

FIGURE 4.1. Phase 1 of the CBE process of inquiry: Fact finding.

This prior knowledge barrier is sometimes referred to as the "tomato effect"—rejecting an efficacious treatment because of prior misinformation (Goodwin & Goodwin, 1984). It is called this because when European explorers first encountered tomatoes in the New World, they correctly recognized them as a relative of deadly nightshade—which (as you can probably tell from the name) is highly toxic. The assumption was that *any* type of nightshade must be toxic, and this misinformation was passed along for decades until someone ate a tomato without ill effects. In Chapter 2 we discussed some of the common educational misconceptions that are often a barrier to accurately identifying a learning problem and therefore implementing effective instruction. There are certainly many others that are commonly or rarely held. It is crucial to be able to step back to identify some of the prior conceptions you are working under in order to know where and when they might function as a barrier to good problem solving.

As we also mentioned earlier, problems that can be identified easily and/or have solutions that can be directly linked to them should be addressed before initiating the CBE process. For example, if a student is squinting when trying to read the board, we assess his eyesight and if acuity is poor, we get him glasses to accommodate his acuity. This is the rule of parsimony.

The reasons for this will be described in more detail in Phase 2: Summative Decision Making when we discuss developing assumed causes, but the point here is that if you are starting the CBE Process to develop a solution to a difficulty a student is having, you should already have a string of documentation of some concern about a problem and various attempts to remedy the difficulty. This process of addressing learning difficulties is a natural part of effective teaching and is sometimes referred to as formative assessment. We constantly need to *differentiate* our instruction to tailor the methods to each student's (or group of students') needs.

> **CBE MAXIM #7:**
>
> **Simple problems don't require complex solutions!**

Concerns about learning can come from a variety of sources. You may have developed the concern based on your interactions with the student. A different educator may have come to you with the concern. The concern may also have come from the student's parents or the student himself. It is important to acknowledge the source of the concern because it can provide a useful piece of information later in the process such as under what conditions the learning problem is demonstrated, if it is related to other setting characteristics, or the role of different expectations and perceptions of student performance.

Identifying that we have a concern about a student's learning should be a quick determination. It does not need to be specific, and as in brainstorming sessions where every idea is shared and then considered, every concern about learning should be considered. Within the fact-finding phase, it is possible that the concern that was initially considered is eased because it was:

- A difference in perception or expectation that, once clarified, removed the concern,
- Not as complex as initially thought (and therefore has a simple solution), or
- Based on faulty information or a misconception.

So whenever there is a concern that appears to warrant CBE, Phase 1 should be used to determine next steps or rule out the need for them. No matter the source of the concern about the learning of a student or group of students, it should lead directly to developing a clear definition of the problem.

ACTION 1.2: DEFINE THE PROBLEM

Because the action of defining the problem is the basis for the rest of the fact-finding phase, it constitutes a rather high-stakes action—if we do not do this accurately and exercise good judgment, everything else we do will be misaligned with the problem.

So the first determination must be where the problem resides—is the problem specific to this student, an entire class, an entire grade, or a group of students? The reason this is so

CBE MAXIM #8:

Always check your alignment!

important is that if the problem is common across students across an entire grade within a school, but we treat it as an individual student problem, it might help that student, but will leave a lot of other students behind—when it might have been more efficient and effective to provide something to everyone who needed it. If five of your 20 students need more intensive reading intervention, you aren't going to pull them out individually and do the same thing; you are going to set up a small-group intervention where you can deliver the same thing once (rather than five times) and also build on cooperative learning, varied opportunities to respond, and all the other excellent strategies that can be used with small groups rather than individual instruction.

Concern was probably initially raised about a student's performance not being sufficient. In order to make sure that's where the appropriate intervention lies, we need to rule out that this student's problem isn't a symptom of a wider issue that is affecting performance across a classroom, grade level, or subgroup of students. In order to make these determinations, you need to have some source of information that:

1. Aligns with the purpose of the decision we are making.
2. Is collected from all students within that grade level.
3. Meets standards of reliability and validity.

The information has to be aligned because, for example, when we want to make a decision about reading, the information had better be about reading. It doesn't make sense to collect information about math to make a decision about reading. We want the information on all students in that grade level for two reasons. First, because the grade is the level of standard to which we are comparing student performance, it makes sense that that is the level we should focus on. Second, we want information on all students because if we don't, we have incomplete information to make the decision. Big threat to good judgment there. The instruments used to collect the information have to be technically sound (i.e., meeting standards of reliability and validity). We discuss issues of reliability and validity in a few other places through this book, but their importance is one reason why we wanted you to make sure you had a solid understanding of the concepts before getting too far into the book. The purpose here is to aggregate data collected from individuals to the classroom or grade level. If the information was collected using different materials or procedures, then our decisions will be faulty because similar reports of performance might mean very different things. This is one of the reasons having good universal screening and meaningful outcome assessment in place is useful. If they are being done well, you have two potential sources of technically sound data that can be aggregated and used to make broader decisions. Data that do not have strong reliability and validity evidence should not be aggregated because that can just magnify the problems. For this step, always use universal screening or outcome assessment results. Let's start by ruling out a problem with the whole grade level.

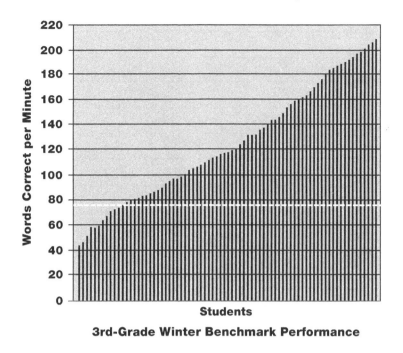

FIGURE 4.2. Gradewide universal screening data illustrating strong performance.

Figure 4.2 shows universal screening data from all four classrooms of a grade level in one elementary school. This is a bar graph (easily created in Excel or any other spreadsheet program that came with your computer) in which the individual students are ranked from lowest score to highest (you can rank high to low if you prefer). It includes third-grade oral passage reading (OPR) data from a winter screening. The horizontal line is the criterion for proficiency (in this case, 77 words read correctly per minute). As can be seen in Figure 4.2, most of the students scored above the criterion for *proficiency* (approximately 86%). In RTI/MTSS, having 80% of students perform above this criterion is a minimum needed to consider the grade level "healthy." This would be considered a positive example because the evidence here suggests that there is no problem specific to the grade level; the majority of students are demonstrating proficiency. Any time you have less than 80% above that line is an indication that there might be a problem at the entire grade level.

The next bar graph (Figure 4.3) gives a slightly different picture. Here only 53% of the students demonstrated proficiency, suggesting that there may be a grade-level problem. It could be a problem with the curriculum coverage, it could be a problem with the scheduling such that there isn't a long enough reading block or too many interruptions occur. There are plenty of conditions at a whole-school or grade level that might be in need of intervention. However, it should also serve as an impetus to look more closely at the classroom data.

Here are the data from Ms. Allen's class (see Figure 4.4). The student she is concerned about is student number 4. We can see that he isn't the lowest-performing student in the class. We can also see that the majority of his classmates are not proficient (only 20% are proficient). Twenty percent proficient is certainly lower than 53% (the grade-level propor-

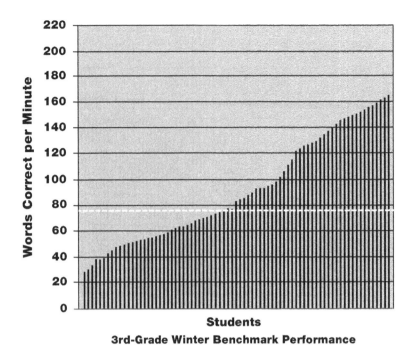

FIGURE 4.3. Gradewide universal screening data illustrating questionable performance.

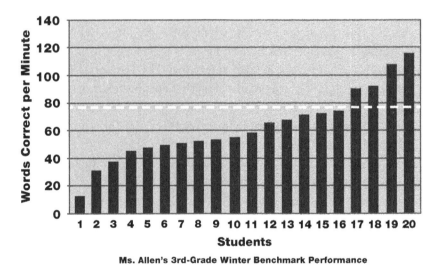

FIGURE 4.4. Classroomwide universal screening data illustrating poor performance.

tion), so it is possible that the problem is at the classroom level. Let's also take a look at these percentages across classrooms.

When we look at the percent proficient in each classroom in that grade level (Figure 4.5), we can see that there are big differences. The first bar in each pair is the percent proficient at the fall screening. At that point each classroom was about 20% proficient. By winter screening, two classrooms stayed about the same, whereas the other two changed dramatically. For the two classrooms that stayed the same, on average the students made typical progress, but stayed behind where they needed to be. For the other two classrooms, these students made excellent progress, with more than 10 students in each classroom moving from "nonproficient" to "proficient." This is the kind of learning we want to see in all classrooms.

From these data, some tentative conclusions we can reach are that the problem does not appear to be specific to the entire grade level, but rather to some classrooms. Student number 4 in Ms. Allen's class is performing similarly to many of his classmates, but he is below the criterion for proficiency. The most reasonable way to intervene here is to provide intervention *at the classroom level*. Once we can demonstrate that the majority of his classmates are learning sufficiently, then we can determine whether he needs something additional in order to learn.

One other decision that can be made looking at the data in this way is to examine them by group of students—particularly for groups of students that might have a different instructional need. For example, Figure 4.6 includes the same data separated by English language learners (ELLs) and fluent English speakers (non-ELLs). It is pretty apparent that the fluent English speakers are doing pretty well, whereas we are not meeting the needs of the ELLs. We probably need to provide more instruction in oral language and supports in their native language to help them build the underlying proficiency and connections.

For the rest of this book, we focus mainly on addressing problems at the individual level. It is what we most often have to do as educators; however, when a problem resides at a level other than the individual student, it is important to make sure that the intervention

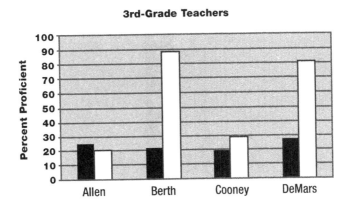

FIGURE 4.5. Cross-classroom universal screening data illustrating varied performance.

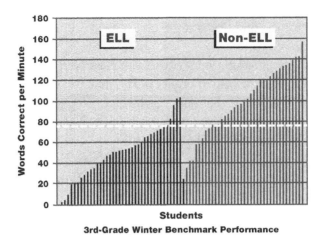

FIGURE 4.6. Universal screening data disaggregated by subgroup to compare performance.

or solution is appropriate for that level. We will provide some examples of these. In essence, the CBE process remains the same as you make decisions, but the alignment of aggregate level (say, the whole class) to the intervention level (making changes in instruction or curriculum that affect the whole class) is a key component to attend to.

In its most simple form, the comparison model as shown in Figure 4.7 is the basis for defining a problem. Within this model, a problem is by definition the difference between performance and a standard. This requires three components: description of student performance, a standard to which to compare student performance, and a criterion for judging the severity of the difference between those two. Action 1.2 will result in a clear statement

FIGURE 4.7. The comparison model.

of performance and the standard. The difference and its severity are verified later once we have collected and summarized the information available.

A good standard is one that is positively stated (explaining what it is the student should be able to do) and includes an action word such as *recites, asks, describes, computes*, or *writes*. This helps to ensure that what we focus our thinking on is observable, measureable, meaningful, and verifiable. But where do standards come from? In English/language arts and mathematics, nearly every state has a core curriculum or state standards. For most states, these are the Common Core State Standards (CCSS; *www.corestandards.org*). They provide a consistent framework for what students should be able to do by the end of each grade level, kindergarten through 12. Chances are you are already familiar with them or will be soon. If so, and if the student's problem is in reading or math, viola! There are your standards. Similar standards for science are also becoming available (*www.nextgenscience.org*). If there are standards or a core curriculum to which all students in your state will be compared, those are the standards to which you should always compare.

However, if there are not clear standards in place in your state, or in the content area in which the student is having the problem, identifying standards becomes a little more difficult. If you are using a set of published curricular materials, chances are that they will have some sort of scope and sequence for the content included and intended to be mastered. Because these standards would align with the materials used to present the content, they would serve as a reasonable substitute for state-adopted standards.

Beyond that, educators are left in a wide-open space. Although it would certainly be possible to set your own standards, the time and effort involved to ensure alignment, evidence base, and meaningfulness in relation to outcomes become prohibitive.

It is also important to identify a standard that is content specific, but not so narrow that it would lead you away from other considerations about the source of difficulty. Remember that this phase of the process is for defining and validating the presence of a problem. If the problem is not accurately validated, alignment is lost and the solutions generated have a lower probability of success. As such, a standard such as "read grade-level text" is probably not detailed enough; however, "identify *r*-controlled vowels within poems" would be too specific. The sweet spot is something that addresses a subdomain of the content area such as one of the five components of reading (phonemic awareness, phonics, fluency, vocabulary, and comprehension) or of math (e.g., operations, geometry, measurement, number sense, algebraic thinking).

The description of the student's performance should be just that: a description of what he can do and how well he does it. It should always be in relation to the action included in the standard. For example, if the standard is to "read with sufficient accuracy and fluency to support comprehension" (which is a standard from the CCSS English/Language Arts for Reading: Foundational Skills at grades 1–5), an appropriate description could be "Hubert reads grade-level text with moderate accuracy, but poor fluency." The description:

- States what he can do (read with moderate accuracy, [read with] poor fluency).
- Includes an action word (*reads*).

There are additional considerations when evaluating a problem definition.

TABLE 4.1. Application of the Dead-Man Test

	Performance definition	Dead-man test
Passes	Billy *reads* grade-level text with moderate accuracy, but poor fluency.	The dead man *reads* grade-level text with moderate accuracy, but poor fluency.
Fails	Billy *cannot read* grade-level material.	The dead man *cannot read* grade-level material.

Evaluating a Problem Definition

A good problem definition will be sufficiently detailed so that:

1. Performance is observable and measureable.
2. The standard is meaningful.
3. The difference is verifiable.

You should evaluate these through the application of some heuristic "tests": the dead man, the "so-what," and the stranger tests.

The **dead-man**[1] **test** is for evaluating the description. It is asking yourself or the team the question "Can a dead man do it?" If the description of the important performance is something that a dead man (under its own power) could "do," then in reality we are not measuring performance but rather the absence of performance. It is more common to make this error with behavioral definitions (e.g., "Hubert does not focus on his work"), but it is still a concern with academic definitions (e.g., "Hubert does not make inferences about what he has read"). The way to apply it is by substituting the term "a dead man" for the student's name in the description.

Table 4.1 illustrates application of the dead man test and contains examples of performance descriptions that pass and fail it using the same example of "Hubert reads grade-level text with moderate accuracy, but poor fluency." As already discussed, the description includes the term "reads" which is an action. Therefore "a dead man" cannot perform the action. As illustrated in the second row of Table 4.1, any definition with a "not," "can't," or "doesn't" is likely to fail. When the description is to *not* perform the action, a dead man can do it.

The **"so-what" test** is important to evaluating the meaningfulness of the standard. If you have taken the standard to which the student's performance is to be compared directly from the state-adopted guidelines, there is a degree of meaningfulness there. At the end of the course or grade level, the student's performance will be compared to that standard through some assessment and evaluation mechanism (whether it is a test, a performance assessment, or a grade). It has a potential impact on that student and his education as well as his life (which is high stakes indeed).

---

[1]This is a long-established standard. If you are uncomfortable with use of the term "dead man," feel free to use the term "a mannequin" instead. It has the same effect.

If you do not have state-adopted standards or a core curriculum to use, the so-what test becomes a little trickier. If using a scope and sequence included within curricular materials, that standard has clear meaning within those materials, but it may not be known how well it generalizes outside of those materials. A well-crafted set of materials will provide the users with references to the empirical studies justifying inclusion of the standards so that you can judge for yourself. When developing standards that are not state adopted or included within the curricular materials, that empirical justification is up to you to find. There are places to go for help (such as the What Works Clearinghouse or the Center on Instruction websites; see the Resources section at the end of the book), but even then it involves greater effort. We recommend only doing this if the other options aren't available.

The *stranger test* can be used to evaluate whether the description is observable, measurable, and meaningful, all of which is encompassed in the ability to verify the difference between standard and performance and therefore the definition of the problem. The stranger test involves having a colleague read your description to determine whether she could determine a way to observe and measure the student's performance and judge the standard for meaningfulness. It is important to note that your description probably isn't so detailed that your colleague would use the same materials you would. She may recommend test B, whereas you were thinking of test A. As long as she would arrive at a similar approach and the two methods essentially measure the same thing, your description has received stranger approval.

Note that the stranger test requires having someone else read the description. This brings up two cautions. First, make sure that the "stranger" is someone you know, trust, and is also an educator with the requisite background knowledge to make informed judgments and recommendations. Second, be aware of student privacy and confidentiality rights (the Family Educational Rights and Privacy Act [FERPA], also known as the Buckley amendment). If the colleague works in your school and also works with the student, she may have good reason to know the information. If she does not work in your school, it is less likely that she has reason to know. To be sure, you should leave the student's name and any other potentially identifying information off.

Again, because the stranger test has someone else reading the description, it means that a different individual or group could use it as a starting point for the CBE process. They could also conduct the rest of the actions of Phase 1 to arrive at the same logical conclusion you did—that the problem was verified or not. To maximize the chance of them reaching the same conclusion, having explicit criteria by which to judge student performance is necessary.

Define the Criteria for Judging the Severity of the Difference

The explicit level of performance used to evaluate whether the student's performance meets the standard is called the *criterion of acceptable performance* (CAP). It is ideal that the CAP is empirically derived—that research was done to determine that this level of performance either (1) leads to certain outcomes with a specified level of probability, or (2) predicts a meaningful level of performance on a criterion measure with a specified level of probability. High-stakes tests have a CAP, the point above which a student's performance is judged to be proficient. Often these are determined through a content review, expert consensus, or a normative referent such as the 40th percentile. When a CAP like this exists on a high-stakes test to which the student will be compared, it makes for a meaningful outcome. However, high-stakes tests and these levels of performance are generally in pretty broad areas (e.g., reading, mathematics, or science) that do not provide additional leads for more detailed definition. In addition, you don't want to define a problem based on one source of information. Therefore, the CAP for other sources of information should also be empirically derived, but this probably leaves you with the question: Just what does ***empirically derived*** mean anyway?

For a good, empirically derived CAP, you want to see that someone has conducted research that meets certain standards of rigor (various organizations have developed these standards and will apply them to judge research studies). For CAP, this research should:

- Use a large and diverse enough group of students to reach generalized conclusions.
- Demonstrate that the instruments were administered with fidelity.
- Compare performance to an appropriate criterion measure.
- Use statistical analysis designed to identify the level of performance required to predict proficiency on the criterion measure.

Although norms (such as the 40th percentile) can be appropriate for a high-stakes test because that is what the state has set as the bar for proficiency, norms are rarely appropriate for other instruments to predict that outcome. Norms provide a description of relative standing in comparison to a group—either the one on which the test was developed (the standardization group) or a local group (local norms). Just because Hubert did better than 40% of that group, doesn't mean that he is proficient at the task; nor does it mean that he isn't proficient at the task. Hubert's score at the 40th percentile only means that that score is as good as or better than 40% of the referent group's scores. What you want to use as a CAP is a criterion-referenced cut score, also sometimes called a benchmark. This is the point on a performance distribution at which the student has a certain probability of performing above the criterion for proficiency on the outcome measure.

ACTION 1.3: COLLECT EXISTING INFORMATION

In order to sufficiently define the problem, it is important to know all the facts. In order to do that we have to have a systematic way of collecting and summarizing what we have and know. As you can attest, a plethora of information is available to us as educators. Much of it you will already be aware of—particularly since you probably collected it! This gives that information salience—a threat to good judgment in that the information can seem more important because it is easier to remember or recall (refer back to Table 2.1). Although it is important to include, it is also important to make sure to include information from other sources.

In Chapter 1, we mentioned the RIOT assessment procedures: ***Review, Interview, Observe, Test.*** These are four different categories of data collection procedures. At this point in the CBE process, we will mostly be reviewing what has already been collected. However, it is important to consider reviewing information that has already been collected through interview, observation, and testing. One reason for this is that it is possible to get different information or different perspectives on the information using different procedures. Consider three different sources of information about a student's reading in Table 4.2.

Our student, Hubert, and his teacher, Ms. Smedley, were both asked about reading. Hubert gave information about his perceptions of and his skills in reading. Ms. Smedley provided information about Hubert's motivation or effort and instructional characteristics. Someone also observed Hubert in Ms. Smedley's class and determined that he pays attention and tries hard. Last, Hubert was given a CBM of second-grade reading passages. His performance was compared to a standard and determined to be well below proficiency (42 words correct per minute with a benchmark of 72 for his grade at this time of year). We have information about Hubert's metacognition ("I have trouble sometimes") from interviewing him, his conceptual knowledge ("He has trouble monitoring his word recognition and decoding") from interviewing his teacher, his metacognition (attends well and engages) from observing him, and his skill performance (42 words correct per minute) from the CBM.

"Where Can I Find Existing Information That Is Relevant?"

The most important thing to consider is that, first, you want to collect readily available information. Form 4.1 provides a general checklist for desired sources. At a minimum, you should attempt to access each of these sources although some may not be available. For example, a student may not have an individualized education plan (IEP) or Section 504 (Americans with Disabilities Act) plan. External reports may not be available, particularly if the student has not had an evaluation by a psychologist, occupational therapist, or other specialist. Universal screening data won't be available if your school doesn't collect it, and

TABLE 4.2. Different Procedures to Collect Information about Hubert's Computation Skills

Procedure	Information
Interview	Hubert: I like reading. It's fun, but I have trouble sometimes.
	Ms. Smedley: Hubert tries very hard, but he's having trouble monitoring his word recognition and decoding.
Observe	Hubert attends well during reading instruction and engages with the teacher and other students.
Test	Hubert can read 42 words correct per minute on second-grade reading passages, which is below the benchmark of 72.

Checklist for Reviewed Sources

Directions: Each of the following information sources should be sought and reviewed.
Check which were reviewed or provide a brief reason why it was not.

Information Source	Reason for Not Reviewing
☐ Cumulative folder	
☐ Universal screening data	
☐ Progress monitoring data	
☐ End of grade/course test scores (e.g., statewide tests)	
☐ Health, vision, hearing screening results	
☐ Report cards	
☐ Work samples	
☐ Interview with current/previous teacher(s)	
☐ Interview parent(s)/student	
☐ Classroom observation	
☐ Intervention plans and reports	
☐ External reports (physicians, psychologists, physical therapist, etc.)	
☐ IEP, IFSP, 504 plan	
☐ Other (please specify)	

interviewing the previous teacher won't work well if the student recently moved to your school.

A thorough review of the information and documentation that does exist and can be examined provides a solid foundation. At the very least, every student must have: a cumulative folder; work samples; health, vision, and hearing screening results; and the potential to interview the parent/guardian and/or student. If the student is not new to your school, there will also be report cards, universal screening, and/or end-of-year test results. In addition, this probably is not the first time concern has been raised about the student's learning. There should be documentation about what has been used with the student in the past and how well it worked. Any other documentation from a grade-level team, professional learning community, or individual teacher's own alterations to instruction should be accessed.

At this point, you want to consider any piece of information, but it is important to remember that ultimately we want to focus on alterable variables because they are relevant for planning instruction, which ultimately is what leads to learning. Although the student growing up in an impoverished environment could have a negative effect on his learning, this is not something that we as educators can change. It would not lead us to choose one instructional strategy over another or affect any of the characteristics of effective instruction. Therefore, you want to look for sources that provide direct information about the things we need to think about.

Evaluation Domains

One thing you typically will observe when looking at the documentation is that most of it focuses on the student. The initial concern was about the student's learning, but learning does not occur in isolation. Learning is an interaction among several domains, and as such, a learning problem can occur in any one or in the interactions among them. Which brings us to CBM Maxim #9.

When collecting the relevant existing information, it is important to think more broadly than just details about the student. Information that can be helpful in planning and evaluating instruction fall within four different evaluation domains:

> **CBE MAXIM #9:**
>
> **Learning problems don't always reside within the learner!**

1. *Setting:* the educational environment.
2. *Curriculum:* what we teach and expect the student to learn.
3. *Instruction:* how we teach the curriculum to the student.
4. *Learner:* the student.

Collectively these are the **SCIL evaluation domains.** Going back to the example of Hubert and his difficulty with reading, it is certainly possible that the difficulty stems from some prerequisite knowledge that Hubert has not yet mastered (this is the focus of Chapter 5 on Phase 2: Summative Decision Making). Yet in order for us to make that determination, we must rule out the setting, curriculum, or instruction as the source of the problem.

Form 4.2 can be used in the process of reviewing the existing relevant data. Each source will yield information that can go into one or more of the SCIL rows. It isn't important to classify what assessment procedure was used to collect the information because at this point we are reviewing existing documents. By clearing the checklist in Form 4.1, you will make sure that interviewing, observing, and testing were all considered and represented.

Let's walk through some sources and where the information they yield might fall. The cumulative folder will contain a lot of learner information such as demographics and attendance, as well as if he has moved schools or repeated grades. Universal screening data, high-stakes test results, health/vision/hearing screening results, and report cards will all yield learner-specific information.

Interviews with the student's teachers, either current or previous, can provide learner information that can be compared to other sources such as tests. They can also provide information about the instruction, curriculum, and setting. Questions should revolve around instructional characteristics such as pacing, strategies and methods used, and frequency and duration of instructional sessions. Curricular areas asked about should include the materials used, content emphasis (phonics, comprehension, computation, writing, geometry), and sequence of presentation. Setting variables might include room arrangement, rules and classroom management plan, and use of grouping.

Parent and student interviews will probably be similar, and should cover the same information since it is a good way to corroborate other sources or compare perceptions. These are also good sources of information about issues that might be context specific. The student interview can also help to identify patterns of motivation and self-awareness.

Classroom observations can be structured in different ways to gather information about different domains. The most common approaches focus on the learner (including effort, attention to task, and social interactions) or the instruction (including pacing, teacher–student interaction, and opportunities for practice and feedback). Curriculum characteristics are often included with instructional emphasis observations. However, there are also specific observation protocols to use for observing the classroom environment (i.e., the setting). It is important to be clear about the purpose of the observation in order to determine which protocol to use or what to focus on during the observation.

The last group of sources includes ones that will be less frequently available. If a student has previously received special education services, there might be an IEP or individualized family service plan (IFSP) available. There might also be a Section 504 plan to cover accommodations that did not warrant special education services. Related to these are reports from professionals external to the school that might be available. For example, the student's parents may have shared the report from their pediatrician, a clinical psychologist, speech–language pathologist, or physical therapist. A report may exist from any specialist who has evaluated or worked with the student on an educationally relevant skill.

"When Do I Have Enough Information to Make a Decision?"

As we discussed in Chapter 2, good judgment depends on having the right information, but also having the right *amount* of information. Too little information increases the threat of

The RIOT/SCIL Matrix to Review Existing Information

Setting	☐ Review	
	☐ Interview	
	☐ Observe	
	☐ Test	
Curriculum	☐ Review	
	☐ Interview	
	☐ Observe	
	☐ Test	
Instruction	☐ Review	
	☐ Interview	
	☐ Observe	
	☐ Test	
Learner	☐ Review	
	☐ Interview	
	☐ Observe	
	☐ Test	

poor decisions because you are likely missing an important piece of information. Using the Checklist of Reviewed Sources (Form 4.1) will help combat having too little information by ensuring that you have considered what is already available. But what to do about having too much information?

Something to be aware of when reviewing existing data is *saturation*—the point at which you have collected enough information to maximize the probability of making a good decision. It can be thought of as the point of diminishing returns where collecting additional information will not add as much to your probability as it does take up valuable time and resources. For better or worse, there is no metric for determining when you have reached the point of saturation (it's not like we can measure data in decibels or gallons). As such, it is a conceptual point. If you use the Checklist of Reviewed Sources, the next step should be to summarize the information in order to take full stock of what is known and unknown. This can help you decide whether you have enough information.

ACTION 1.4:
SUMMARIZE INFORMATION

Once you have reviewed the records and collected the first wave of information into the RIOT/SCIL matrix, the next step is to distill this information into a more manageable format. In essence, this is done by doing three different things: aggregating, asking, and answering.

First, you want to aggregate the information that you have. By filling in the RIOT/SCIL matrix, you have already put the information at hand into an aggregate format. However, you will probably find that it is a *lot* of information. Skim the information in the RIOT/SCIL matrix and identify the three most important pieces within each of the evaluation domains. These should be transferred to Form 4.3.

Next you want to ask yourself, "Looking at the information in the RIOT/SCIL matrix, what do I still not know about the setting, curriculum, instruction, and learner?" Like any good detective work, this first step often generates more questions than it answers. You want to think about what else you need to know to make good decisions. While at it, it is important to think about collecting that information using a variety of procedures.

Through this process of aggregating and asking, it is important to consider *disconfirming evidence*—pieces of information that might not align with the pattern of other information. Having disconfirming evidence is a good indication that you are at least close to saturation. Any time you have collected enough information, you will have disconfirming evidence; however, just because you have disconfirming evidence doesn't mean you have collected enough.

If you can't find any disconfirming evidence in your RIOT/SCIL matrix, you need to ask yourself why. You should always have some piece of information that doesn't quite fit with the rest because educational problems are rarely (if ever) simple and straightforward. A student who demonstrates a learning problem in one content area, might not show it in another. Other factors may mediate how, when, or to what degree a learning problem is

Unknown Relevant Information to Generate Questions and Guide Decision Making

Evaluation Domain	Relevant Known Information	Relevant Unknown Information	Proposed Procedure (circle all that apply)
Setting		Q1	R I O T
		Q2	R I O T
		Q3	R I O T
Curriculum		Q1	R I O T
		Q2	R I O T
		Q3	R I O T
Instruction		Q1	R I O T
		Q2	R I O T
		Q3	R I O T
Learner		Q1	R I O T
		Q2	R I O T
		Q3	R I O T

manifested. In addition, you should have collected information on other people's perceptions of the learning. So if there is no disconfirming evidence, stop again to ask yourself:

- Is it because there isn't any disconfirming evidence?
  - This is highly unlikely.
  - Solution: go back and check specifically for disconfirming evidence.
- Is it because we didn't look for it?
  - This is possible. It's called selective attention or confirmation bias (refer back to Table 2.1).
  - Solution: go back and check specifically for disconfirming evidence.
- Is it because we looked, but not in the right place or manner?
  - This is likely too. Even when we have been planful in our review, we may have missed it because our focus was on other areas or methods.
  - Solution: go back and check specifically for disconfirming evidence, but this time using different sources or methods.

QUESTION 1: IS THERE A CONFIRMABLE PROBLEM?

This is the "answering" part. You've aggregated the data, asked questions, and now really need to know whether you are comfortable saying that there is a serious problem that needs addressing. There are only two answers to this question: no and yes.

No

If we went through this process and could not confirm the problem, there are four possible reasons:

1. The student does not really have a problem.
2. The definition of the problem is not specific enough or accurate.
3. The standard for comparison is not appropriate.
4. The information used to validate the problem is inappropriate or insufficient.

First, it is possible that when we were ruling out broader problems than one that is student specific, that we discovered a classwide problem with instruction. If that is the case, intervention needs to take place at the classroom level before being able to determine the presence of a student-level problem. It is also possible that the concern about learning was a problem in perception or expectation rather than actual student performance. Although this is not likely to be the only source of concern (even with differences in perception or expectation, there is some standard of performance that is being used and must misalign in some way), it is important to examine if the problem was not confirmed.

Second, it is possible that, in the act of defining the problem, we were not accurate in narrowing down the prime content area or missed the possibility of a different source that might affect multiple content areas or broader levels such as the classroom or grade level. It is also possible that we were not specific enough in our definition to guide our thinking and data collection through the rest of our fact finding.

Third, we might be comparing the student's performance to an inappropriate standard. If external grade-level standards exist (such as the CCSS), we need to make sure that we are using appropriate standards and CAPs for the student's grade level. If Hubert is in second grade, but we know his instructional level in reading is first grade, he still needs to be compared to the second-grade standards using appropriate materials. Deciding that second-grade Hubert doesn't have a problem in reading because he met the standard for the first-grade materials with which he is being taught will mask the problem of Hubert being below proficiency.

Last, we might have used insufficient or inappropriate information. Despite our adherence to the checklist, other sources might exist. When identifying the most important pieces, maybe we fell into the trap of one of the threats to good judgment and gave more importance to something than we should have. We also could have discounted some information because it did not agree with other information, and rather than working to account for it, we ignored it. The information could also be inappropriate because it was not collected or reported properly. The best thinking will still lead to faulty decisions if we are basing it on poor information such as data collected without fidelity or violating standardization, for purposes for which it is not valid, or based on perceptions and opinion.

Yes

If we are able to confirm that there is a problem and that the severity is such that it warrants further evaluation and intervention, then it is time to move from Phase 1: Fact Finding, to Phase 2: Summative Decision Making.

CHAPTER SUMMARY

In this chapter, we presented the first phase of the CBE process in greater detail. This phase of fact finding sets the stage for the more detailed thinking required for determining the source of the problem as well as generation and implementation of a solution. Concern about a student's learning is common; however, there are many threats to good judgment that can interfere with our taking the time to consider what we know and how we know it. This process is essential for solving the most complex problem, because if a simple solution existed, we certainly would have tried it without going through the steps of collecting and evaluating additional information. Once we have uncovered the information we need and verified that there is a problem in need of solution, it is time to move on to the more detailed work of examining why that problem exists.

CHAPTER 5

CBE Process Phase 2
Summative Decision Making

In the previous chapter, we did our fact-finding "legwork" by bringing together everything that we know about a student instructionally so that we have a solid foundation of information. Some of that information was determined to be nonessential because it relates to nonalterable things, but much of it is about things that are alterable and important. While collecting the existing information (and probably even before that), you were generating hypotheses about what the problem is and how to fix. Don't try to hide it. Like us, you went into education because you wanted to help students learn. We do that by teaching. So when a student is having difficulty learning, that's when we get to do our best teaching! We've already thought about potential problems and solutions.

SOME WORDS OF CAUTION

One of the most common errors we see is educators moving directly from confirming the presence of a problem (Phase 1) directly to trying to solve the problem (Phase 3). There should be very few times when this is a good idea, much less a successful one. For simple problems that don't require systematic approaches to decision making like CBE, this can work. However, when the problem is complex it can actually cost a lot of time and resources due to falling into the trap of one of the threats to good judgment presented in Chapter 2. You have already determined that the problem is significant, and you have already tried some simpler solutions in addition to ruling out problems that actually reside at broader levels such as the entire classroom or grade level. When a solution to a problem can be generated from the information reviewed within the process of fact finding, one of three things happened:

1. Complex decision-making procedures were used for a simple problem.
2. There was already good information that led to a solution, but it was not being used.
3. Poor (or misaligned) information was used to develop a solution.

None of these options are indications of the CBE process going awry per se; they are indications of a system-level problem. The problem might be that there is not a consistent process for using data to make decisions, which would allow for simple or straightforward problems to be missed. It could also be that appropriate data are not being collected or summarized for decision making or that sufficient procedures are not used for protecting against threats to good judgment.

If skipping Phase 2 leads to resolution of the student-level problem, it is an indication of a system-level problem—either in professional development, decision making processes, or application of the decision making. If skipping Phase 2 doesn't lead to resolution, an error obviously occurred and the time spent in Phase 3 will largely have been wasted because now we need to go back to Phase 2. This leads to CBM Maxim #10.

The reason CBE is systematic is to increase the probability of making good inferences that lead to positive outcomes. In the day-to-day work of trying to help all of our students, it is easy to fall into simple traps in thinking, and our prior knowledge makes them seem appropriate even when

> **CBE MAXIM #10:**
>
> **Sometimes the greatest barrier to problem solving is prior knowledge!**

they aren't. There's a common saying that "When you have a hammer, everything looks like a nail." This is the threat of familiarity. Every reading problem should be solved using the same strategy or approach. Any time a student has difficulty attending to tasks he must have ADHD. Going through the steps of generating and testing assumed causes of student learning problems will make it less likely that the easiest or closest-at-hand solution will be the one always leaned on, and the most effective or best aligned with student need option will.

THE PURPOSE OF PHASE 2: SUMMATIVE DECISION MAKING

Whereas Phase 1 is most closely aligned with the types of educational decisions one would associate with screening, Phase 2 is much more about *diagnostic decisions* (Hosp, 2011). If you're having car trouble, your first approach is probably to make sure it isn't something simple like needing more gas, inflating the tires, or adding oil. However, if you do those things and find that your car still isn't running properly, you're likely to take it to a mechanic.

The mechanic will ask you some questions about what the problem is, have you make the sound several times for comedic effect (*brah-yuk, brah-yuk, clang, clang, clang*), and may come up with a hypothesis. If the problem is that your car isn't running smoothly and doesn't seem to have its usual amount of power, he may hypothesize that it is the alternator. If he's a good mechanic, his next step is not to grab a brand-new alternator, install it in your car, and charge you $600. His next step is to rule out other, simpler explanations: Can the battery hold a charge? Are the belts in good condition? Are bearings and connections lubricated and not worn? These would be prerequisites to replacing an alternator. In addition, he can run certain tests to make sure the battery is okay and the alternator itself is functioning.

Your mechanic ultimately wants a resolution to the problem—that your car is running smoothly again. However, he also wants to make sure that the solution is appropriate, such as replacing the belts if they were the problem rather than replacing the alternator and then the belts. He knows that he can't just start replacing parts until he finds the one that is faulty. He must be planful in his approach to find the most effective and efficient solution. That isn't to say that he will find the problem the first time every time, but he will increase his chances.

It works pretty much the same way in education. When we have confirmed that Hubert has a learning problem, we don't just start teaching him different things in different ways to try to find the right one. We also don't just use whatever is closest or most convenient (imagine if your mechanic used a wrench for everything because of the portability). We need to figure out what Hubert needs in order to determine the most effective and efficient way to teach him what he has not yet mastered. The way to do that is to generate assumed causes and work toward validating them (see Figure 5.1).

ACTION 2.1: GENERATE ASSUMED CAUSES

In Phase 1 we determined that the student is struggling. This is our chance to figure out why. At this point, we are still working with the information reviewed in the RIOT/SCIL matrix. There is a lot of information there. We should document what we think might be the source of the student's difficulty. In addition to the RIOT/SCIL matrix, it is necessary to have a clear set of standards or prerequisite skills against which we compare the student's performance. Based on the comparison of the student's performance to the standards, we need to generate statements about:

1. Which skills the student has mastered.
2. Which skills are emerging.
3. Which skills are unknown.

Mastered skills are success stories. We don't need to teach them, and the student doesn't need much practice either. An emerging skill is one that the student knows how to do, but might not be able to do with sufficient accuracy or fluency. The student likely requires varying amounts of guided or independent practice, but probably only some instruction to reinforce the skill. Unknown skills are ones that clearly need to be taught because the student does not yet know how to do them. The statements of emerging and unknown skills will become the basis for generating *assumed causes.*

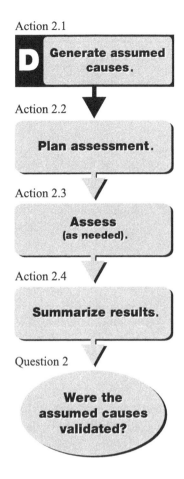

Action 2.1

D **Generate assumed causes.**

Action 2.2

Plan assessment.

Action 2.3

Assess (as needed).

Action 2.4

Summarize results.

Question 2

Were the assumed causes validated?

FIGURE 5.1. Phase 2 of the CBE process of inquiry: Summative decision making.

Rules for Developing Assumed Causes

When generating assumed causes, following certain rules will increase the odds of verifying the assumed causes. These are shown in Table 5.1. Assumed causes should be observable and measureable, and should hold up to the same tests for problem definitions (i.e., the dead-man, so-what, and stranger tests). This is because we are going to test these hypotheses in order to justify the direction we take when planning the intervention to solve the student's learning problem. If the assumed cause is not a testable hypothesis with clear potential for verification, it won't provide the foundation for intervention planning because, at best, it will be a hunch.

An assumed cause should always be a skill that is a *prerequisite* to the one the student has not yet mastered. That way, once that assumed-cause skill is mastered, our instruction moves on to the next skill in the sequence until the student is at his grade-appropriate level. In any good skill sequence or set of standards, each one is an action. This ensures that each skill is alterable—if it is an action we can watch a student perform, it can be performed with varying degrees of proficiency, and it can be taught!

TABLE 5.1. Rules for Developing Assumed Causes

Rule	Explanation
1. Focus on alterable skills.	Alterable skills are ones that we can teach to a student. If we can't change it through instruction, then the solution lies outside the educational system.
2. Stick to essential tasks.	Just because something is alterable, doesn't mean that it is important for us to teach. If it isn't included in the standards or a prerequisite to a standard, it is probably not essential.
3. Prioritize problems.	Complex problems generally include multiple facets. Focus on the skills that will facilitate learning others.
4. Pick the most likely targets first.	Rule out the common problem causes before more exotic or rare ones.
5. Use skill sequences.	Every skill has prerequisite skills and also serves as a prerequisite to other skills. Priority should be given to skills earlier in the sequence.

A caveat to this focus is that, just because something can be changed and therefore taught, doesn't make it important to do so. Skills within the standards or curricular sequence are probably a safe bet to be essential because they are ones that (at least in theory, if not actual testing practice) the student is expected to master by the end of his grade or course. It is also important to be aware that because Hubert is exhibiting a complex problem, there is probably more than one essential skill he has not yet mastered. This makes it important to prioritize the problems as well as the assumed causes. The highest-priority skills are ones that are:

> **CBE MAXIM #11:**
>
> **If you can't change it, don't assess it!**

1. Essential skills themselves.
2. A foundation for other essential skills, and
3. Early in the skill sequence.

An essential skill that is considered a standard or outcome at one grade level, but a prerequisite at another, is sometimes called a *tool skill*. A general example is accurate and fluent reading. In grades 1–5, this is a standard in the CCSS for English language arts. There are many prerequisite skills to accurate and fluent reading (that involve concepts of print, phonemic awareness, alphabetic knowledge). However, in middle and high school accurate and fluent reading becomes a tool skill in the content areas because it is a way to access the content. One cannot understand and apply biology content in an inquiry-based format without the skill to access that content in written form. And imagine trying to understand European history without being able to read a history book (no, you can't wait for the movie).

TABLE 5.2. Examples of Good and Poor Assumed Cause Generation

	Fact	Assumed cause	Test	Result
Example	Hubert computes mixed math problems with 45% accuracy.	Difficulty selecting appropriate operation to use	Knowledge of operations	Hubert confuses addition and multiplication signs.
Nonexample	Hubert computes mixed math problems with 45% accuracy.	Low logical–mathematical intelligence	Cognitive processing or aptitude	Hubert is incapable of mastering this content.

To illustrate this, Table 5.2 includes a positive example and one of faulty assumed cause generation. The first example stays within the skill sequence, focusing on something that is essential and alterable—whether Hubert can determine when to apply certain mathematical operations. The faulty assumed cause has moved outside the skill sequence to something that is not alterable, such as innate or fixed ability.[1] Because it is outside the skill sequence, it is not essential. Because it is not alterable, it cannot be taught. Even if we were to verify this as an assumed cause, it is not something Ms. Smedley can use to plan instruction and would be frustrating for her because it will take precious time away from teaching the things that she *can* teach.

An Example

Let's walk through an example to help us think about which skills, what sequence, and which are necessary in terms of learning more complex skills versus which don't need to be focused on (at least for the time being). Recall that Ms. Smedley confirmed Hubert's problem with reading in that he cannot read grade-appropriate text with sufficient accuracy or fluency (CCSS Standard RF 2.4). This makes her think that Hubert is having trouble with decoding because he cannot do it quickly or accurately. She also noted that he did not self-correct any of his mistakes. Looking at the CCSS under Reading: Foundational Skills, she first looks at the skills under Standard RF 2.4 (Fluency). They are:

a. Read grade-level text with purpose and understanding.
b. Read grade-level text orally with accuracy, appropriate rate, and expression.
c. Use context to confirm or self-correct word recognition and understanding, rereading as necessary.

She notes that he has demonstrated an understanding of different purposes of text and generally selects text appropriate for the purposes. Skill b is what triggered her concerns in

---

[1]Remember back in Chapter 2 when we discussed key educational misconceptions that will derail the instructional process? Here's one way they do that.

the first place because his oral reading is inaccurate and slow. However, given that he did not self-correct while reading the passage and his accuracy was low (indicating that there was ample opportunity and need to self-correct), she suspects that this might be an important skill to consider. This isn't a prerequisite to accurate and fluent reading, though. Being able to read accurately without the need to self-correct very often is a stronger demonstration of reading grade-appropriate text accurately and fluently than having to interrupt the pace of reading by having to reread often.

To look for additional prerequisite skills, she focuses on the previous standard under Reading: Foundational Skills, Standard RF 2.3: Phonics and Word Recognition. The skills under this standard are:

a. Distinguish long and short vowels when reading regularly spelled one-syllable words.
b. Know spelling–sound correspondences for additional common vowel teams.
c. Decode regularly spelled two-syllable words with long vowels.
d. Decode words with common prefixes and suffixes.
e. Identify words with inconsistent but common spelling–sound correspondences.
f. Recognize and read grade-appropriate irregularly spelled words.

This is a running list of phonics and word analysis skills all students should be able to do by the end of second grade. The order in which they appear can be seen as an increase (moving up alphabetically) in the complexity, which provides a sequence in which to teach skills. From the examination of his screening data as well as other work samples, Ms. Smedley noticed that Hubert's errors seem to be predominantly words with prefixes and suffixes as well as irregularly spelled words. Because neither of these skills is a prerequisite for the other (grade-appropriate irregularly spelled words do not necessarily contain prefixes or suffixes), Ms. Smedley feels that both are potential assumed causes for Hubert's inaccurate and slow reading. These cover the within-grade skills to examine and provide her with a good place to start. If she was being thorough (and we hope she would be), she would also ensure that Hubert had mastered Skills a–c, which are prerequisites to Skill d because they all address skills involved in the root of a word, whereas Skill d focuses on the affixes that are added on to the root.

Another area to examine is previous grade-level skills. Standards should generally be linked not only within grade, but across grades, with skills building from one year to the next. As such, this year's skills are next year's prerequisites. Therefore, if a student has difficulty with this year's skills, its prerequisites would include last year's skills.

F.AC.T.R.

One thing you may have noticed about Table 5.2 is that there were several columns in addition to the assumed cause. Like almost everything else in this book, the process of developing and verifying assumed causes can be covered by a worksheet or checklist. In this case, that is the F.AC.T.R. worksheet (Form 5.1). The acronym stands for Fact–Assumed Cause–

F.AC.T.R. Worksheet

Student name: **Date:**

Directions: Complete each section.

Fact	Assumed Cause	Test	Results
The standard that the student is not performing proficiently	The prerequisite skill causing the problem	How to assess the prerequisite skill	Has the student mastered the prerequisite skill?

Test–Result. The procedures for working through this sheet include stating the clearly defined problem (the fact) and then the hypothesized reason (the assumed cause). The fact should be stated as the difference between the CAP on the standard and the student's actual performance (refer back to Figure 4.7). This not only indicates what the problem is, but also shows the magnitude of the problem. If any of the steps of F.AC.T.R. can't be fit into the worksheet, there is a problem with the process. It could be that the assumed cause is too detailed to have instructional utility (for example, Hubert cannot read words with an *r*-controlled letter *e* in the rime of the first syllable of two-syllable words when preceded by the letter digraph *ph*). It may also be that the assumed cause is outside the skill sequence or standards and alignment have been lost.

If multiple problems are present, then assumed causes should be developed for each one. In addition, it is likely that multiple assumed causes can be developed for each problem. If there are multiple likely causes, then each one should be tested to determine which is the actual cause or whether the problem has multiple sources. Once the fact and assumed cause(s) are included into the F.AC.T.R. worksheet, the rest of the sheet is completed in the following actions as we determined how we will measure the performance of the assumed cause (the test) and compare that to a criterion for performing it proficiently so that we can determine whether it may be causing the problem (the result).

Let's consider Hubert. During our process of fact finding, we determined that Hubert's reading of grade-level text is both inaccurate and too slow. This falls under the CCSS Standard Reading: Foundational Skills, Fluency (RF 2.4). Ms. Smedley notes:

> *Fact*: "Hubert read 42 words correctly per minute (of 80 attempted, 52.5% accuracy) from second-grade passages, which is well below his grade-level cut score for the winter benchmark (72 WCPM)."

Because Hubert is both inaccurate and not fluent, Ms. Smedley hypothesized that his difficulty might lie with his application of grade-level decoding skills. This is the previous standard within the CCSS, Reading: Foundational Skills, Phonics and Word Recognition (RF 2.3a–f). In particular, he might have difficulty recognizing and reading grade-appropriate irregularly spelled words (RF 2.3f) or decoding words with common prefixes and suffixes (RF 2.3d). She also hypothesized that it could be difficulty using context to confirm or self-correct word recognition that is affecting his reading. This is a concurrent skill (RF 2.4c) within the standard he has not yet mastered—Reading: Foundational Skills, Fluency. This left her with three assumed causes for the fact of inaccurate and slow reading:

> *Assumed Cause #1*: Hubert cannot accurately and fluently read grade-appropriate irregularly spelled words.
>
> *Assumed Cause #2*: Hubert cannot accurately and fluently decode words with common prefixes and suffixes.
>
> *Assumed Cause #3*: Hubert cannot use context to confirm or self-correct word recognition.

Notice that Ms. Smedley used the rules from Table 5.1. The skills addressed in these assumed causes are alterable, essential and sequenced (they are included in the standards), and prioritized and likely (they are proximal to the difficulty Hubert is having).

ACTION 2.2: PLAN ASSESSMENT

Like every action in the CBE process, plan assessment depends on what occurred in the actions before it. The assessment procedures we use here are directly aligned with the assumed causes we generated in the last action. At this point, we are figuring out what we need to know to verify or rule out the assumed cause. If we used appropriate skill sequences and stuck to essential skills, the assessment plan should be clear. Just as there were rules for *developing* the assumed causes that make the process more systematic and increase the probability of accurate outcomes, there are similar rules for *verifying* the assumed causes. These are shown in Table 5.3.

Because we are using an appropriate skill sequence/set of standards, the skills are, by definition, in a sequence. This sequence is ordered in increasing complexity or to build on prior skills (if it isn't, you should worry). If you think about the skill sequence building that way, as the student moves up in skills (or grades) he gets higher in the sequence. As we are teaching and he is learning, Hubert is growing. Think of this as teaching "up" the sequence. As such, our testing should move down. We start by assessing the student's performance in the most recent or current skill. If he can do that proficiently, there is no problem—we just need to keep teaching so he keeps learning. But if he can't do that proficiently, we move down to the next prerequisite skill and test that. We continue this process until we find the "highest" skill that Hubert has not yet mastered (this is sometimes referred to as the ***zone of proximal development;*** Vygostky, 1978). This process of test down/teach up is illustrated in Figure 5.2.

TABLE 5.3. Rules for Testing Assumed Causes

Rule	Explanation
1. Test down/teach up.	Test down in the skill sequence to find the most complex skill that isn't mastered yet.
2. Ensure alignment.	Make sure that the source of information is appropriate to provide the information you need.
3. Consider response type.	If you expect a student to produce a response, don't rely on a source that lets him pick from provided options.
4. Consider conditions.	Does the student perform the task differently in isolation rather than in context? Are there different conditions (reading aloud, reading silently) that affect student performance?

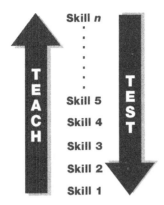

FIGURE 5.2. Test down/teach up through a skill sequence.

An important consideration while testing down is to ensure that how you test student performance on a skill is aligned with the desired performance of that skill. One of the best ways to do this to use a direct measure of the skill. The process for assessing must be appropriate and direct.

A facet of direct alignment is to make sure that you assess the student's response the same way you evaluate his performance. As we discussed in Chapter 2, there are different types of knowledge and different ways of displaying that knowledge. Because good standards and skill sequences use action words, they generally require that the student performs the skill (e.g., accurately and fluently reads grade-appropriate text). As such, you want to use an assessment procedure that requires the student to perform that skill so you can assess it directly. There are ways to assess a student's skill at accurately and fluently reading grade-appropriate text directly (having the student read orally and recording the percent correct and rate of words read correctly) rather than indirectly (having the student read silently and select responses to questions from pre-specified choices). The indirect example is a different skill that requires a different response type. Both are obviously under the broad umbrella of "reading," but remember that we need to be specific and aligned at this stage.

A second facet of direct alignment is to make sure the conditions are consistent. This doesn't mean that the lighting and temperature need to be ideal, but that we are having the student use the appropriate materials. An obvious concern is that the materials we use contain the content that we intend to measure. Assessment of third-grade reading must include text at a third-grade level. Assessment of specific skills must include opportunities to perform those specific skills. There are a variety of other considerations about condition too, such as presentation (oral, written), response (oral, written), and performance in isolation versus in the presence of distractors.

Let's go back to Ms. Smedley and Hubert. In comparing her assumed causes to the standards, Ms. Smedley puts them in an order to "test down" by focusing on assumed cause #3 (self-correction), #1 (irregular words), and then #2 (prefixes and suffixes). She knows that this is not a hard and fast sequence and there is likely a good degree of overlap, especially considering maintenance and generalization during the process of mastering these skills. However, she understands that accurate and fluent reading of grade-appropriate text (with or without self-correction) cannot take place without mastering phonics and word recognition.

Because each of the assumed causes is alterable and observable, she will include assessment procedures that include the actual skills. She will use procedures that require Hubert to perform the task and respond aloud, but realizes that she will need to use different assessment procedures to ensure she has the appropriate information to verify the assumed causes.

ACTION 2.3: ASSESS (AS NEEDED)

For every evaluation question (i.e., for every assumed cause for each confirmed problem) there should be at least one assessment procedure identified to test or confirm the student's performance on that skill. Having more than one assessment procedure allows us to compare different sources that might use different response types or have the student perform the skill under different conditions. This gives us more information to make our decisions.

It is also important to know that some assessment procedures can also address more than one evaluation question. If Hubert's problem is inaccurate computation, diagnostic analysis of mixed math computation probes containing items from Hubert's grade-level standards can provide information about different operations as well as potential information about the types of errors he is making (fact recall, procedural). Verification across multiple sources reinforces the confidence we should have in that assumed cause.

One thing you probably noticed about this action is the parenthetical phrase "(as needed)." Thinking back to our fact finding, you may have wondered why we spent that time pooling all the information at hand into one place. Wonder no more! The vast amount of information we collected means that there may already be sources we can use to verify assumed causes. In essence, there are three potential sources of information for our targeted diagnostic assessment decisions: existing results, reassessing on the same task, or using a new instrument.

Option 1: Existing Results

Depending on the grade level of the student, how long he has been at our school, and the time of year, we will have different amounts of preexisting data from screening and outcome tests, work samples, and results from observations or diagnostic interviews. These are the sources we used to determine that Hubert had a confirmable problem in the first place. Remember that was at a broader level, though. Now that we need to dig deeper into the prerequisite skills that might be causing the problem, we have a different focus. Whereas Ms. Smedley might have looked at Hubert's OPR passages to determine that his reading grade-level text is inaccurate and slow by comparing his performance to empirically derived cut scores, she now looks at her marked-up version of the passages Hubert read. She is looking for evidence of Hubert: (1) self-correcting often or at all, (2) accurately reading grade-appropriate irregularly spelled words, and (3) accurately reading words with common prefixes and suffixes.

One caveat to be aware of here is to not use the same source to generate and verify an assumed cause. It is a surefire way to verify the assumed cause (refer back to those threats to good judgment; this is confirmatory bias). If the determination that Hubert was not accurate at decoding words with common prefixes and suffixes came from the screening data, those same results cannot be used to verify it. Just because Hubert made those errors on this work sample doesn't mean that he will make the same errors again. In particular with reading, errors (also called miscues) are not consistent and provide little diagnostic information (cf. Flynn, Hosp, Hosp, & Robbins, 2011). Errors are more consistent for computation (see Ashlock, 2009), but it is still vital to verify the hypothesis.

A second caveat is that the reliability and validity of an instrument do not hold for this level of analysis. If the existing source is, for example, a reading test that has high reliability and strong validity, the broad decision of whether the student is performing at grade level (for a *criterion-referenced* test) or similarly to peers (for a norm-referenced test) is what those characteristics is associated with. If there are separate subtests, they may have their own reliability and validity evidence; but looking at performance of specific skills is not a level of analysis to which those characteristics generalize. A common misassumption is to overgeneralize good technical characteristics to every piece of a test, but that doesn't hold up at the item or skill level. This is true whether you are reanalyzing the existing results, readministering a test, or giving a new one. It is always important to make sure that the level of analysis aligns with the level at which the reliability and validity were calculated.

> **CBE MAXIM #12:**
>
> **Tools are technically adequate for specific purposes!**

Ms. Smedley had developed her assumed causes based on many sources of information— Hubert's in-class reading performance (where she has listened to him read aloud from grade-appropriate passages), report from parent volunteers and Hubert's own parents, as well as review of Hubert's cumulative folder and comments from his first-grade teacher. She had also looked for these patterns on Hubert's three OPR passages from the winter screening period. It was enough information for her to feel confident that they were assumed causes to be verified, but she did not feel that the information was strong enough or consistent enough to use the existing results as the verification. She decided to explore other assessment options.

Option 2: Reassess on Same Task

One way to combat the potential problem of verifying using the same performance sample as the one you used to generate the assumed causes is to have the student repeat the task using an alternate form of the materials. Because the actual items aren't identical, there shouldn't be a practice effect due to the instrumentation. But if the student is making a discrete and consistent error, it should show up again. This is a process of replication or repeatability.

If we had the student perform the same task again under the same conditions, with the same content, but with different items representing that content, we were able to replicate those errors. This strengthens the argument that this assumed cause is correct. Remember saturation from Phase 1. We want the evidence suggesting the same inference or judgment until we have enough that we are comfortable in verifying that assumed cause.

Just because the errors the student makes the second time aren't exactly the same doesn't mean we haven't gotten verification. It could suggest that it is not a case of the student not being able to perform the skill at all, but rather that the skill is still emerging. Think of the last time you were learning a new skill. Sometimes you were able to perform it quite well and then the very next time, not so much. It takes an awful lot of practice for professional athletes and musicians to be able to perform the same skill the same way over and over. The same thing is true of any academic skill. Pronouncing the word *arachibu-tyrophobia* is very difficult the first several dozen times you said it (especially with peanut butter stuck to the roof of your mouth), but eventually it "rolls off the tongue."

Ms. Smedley considered using other OPR passages because they are aligned, use the same conditions, and use the same response type expected. However, she ultimately decided against it because OPR passages do not provide many opportunities for observing the specific skills she was deciding about, and they are not consistent across passages due to the different content, context, and student prior knowledge. In examining the previous three OPR passages, she identified three grade-appropriate irregularly spelled words. She did not feel that this was sufficient because there are 50 included in the materials of her core curriculum. She also felt that the OPR passages were insufficient for assessing Hubert's use of self-correction while reading because she had noted that he did not self-correct verbally within the standard administration. Ms. Smedley was unsure if this was because he did not use context while reading or whether he did not feel he needed to while performing that task, for example. Last, there were 14 common prefixes and suffixes Hubert attempted across the three passages, but there were no more than two opportunities for each. Overall, Hubert's accuracy with words with prefixes and suffixes was similar to his overall accuracy (55% vs. 52.5%), but she was unsure whether this was a good representation of his decoding words with prefixes and suffixes. Ms. Smedley decided that she needed to use different assessment procedures.

Option 3: Create/Use New Instrument

Sometimes it just isn't possible to use or repeat existing results. When that happens we have to collect new data using a different technique. There are four main reasons why this could happen: low frequency performance, cost, time, and different conditions.

Earlier, when we determined whether a skill was essential, a consideration was whether that skill was a prerequisite to future skills. Because it was, it was essential. However, just because that skill is essential doesn't mean that there are many opportunities for the student to display that skill. If it is a skill that is displayed infrequently, it will be necessary to create a new task or use a premade task for the student that requires him to perform that skill multiple times.

If the existing source is very expensive or time consuming to collect, it would not make much sense to use Option 2. Although we want to be accurate in our verification of the assumed cause, it is important to be efficient. The assumed cause is a specific skill that is displayed during the course of performing the broad skill (reading, math, etc.), so with broad assessment procedures such as end-of-grade tests or extended diagnostic interviews or observations, the skill is likely to be performed, but so are a lot of others. Administering a test or conducting a diagnostic interview/observation that takes 30 to 40 minutes with Hubert to get information about his skill at decoding words with common prefixes and suffixes would be like reading the whole dictionary to find out the definition of the word *Sisyphean*. When you want to know that specific piece of information, you look it up rather than undertaking a seemingly endless and futile quest. The same holds for verifying an assumed cause—find out the specific piece of information you need using procedures that are as direct as possible. Because we are looking at pretty specific skills, the tasks should be relatively short in terms of both items and time required to administer.

In Hubert's case, one way would be to have him read from a list of words with common prefixes and suffixes. Ms. Smedley did just that, creating a standard list using the prefixes and suffixes included in the second-grade materials from her core curriculum using some standard root words from the first-grade core materials. She selected some first-grade words to increase the chance that Hubert could read them, but before creating the materials, she checked to make sure that Hubert could in fact read the root words in isolation. This way, her confidence that errors indicated that Hubert was having difficulty with the prefix or suffix (or the pronunciation changes that come from adding an affix) was increased.

Also consider the assumed cause of recognizing and reading grade-appropriate irregularly spelled words. From his OPR screening results, Ms. Smedley noticed that he had missed two of three opportunities to read irregularly spelled words and that one of those words was taught last year in the core reading series, one this year, and one will be next year. There were not a lot of opportunities for Hubert to demonstrate this skill in those passages. If she were to try to derive this information from existing sources or use alternate forms, it would be time-prohibitive because she would have to listen to Hubert read a lot of grade-appropriate text to ensure that there were multiple opportunities for him to read many of these words. Instead, Ms. Smedley used the list of irregularly spelled words from the second-grade materials from her core curriculum. She also had him read the list from the first-grade materials to check for his maintenance or retention of that skill. If she had him read the same list from the third-grade materials she could get an indication of generalization.

Another reason for needing to use a different task is when you need information about how the student can perform the skill under different conditions. We may have been able to generate an assumed cause from work samples and other assessment results where the student was required to perform the skill in context. This provides the information that the student has not mastered that skill such that he can apply it consistently, but it doesn't tell us much else. Think back to Chapter 2 and the discussion of types of knowledge. With facts and concepts, a student might not be able to recall the information in the presence of distractors (all the other things he must attend to and recall), but could recognize it from a provided list or with a minimal prompt. Teaching that information from scratch is different than helping the student practice or teaching strategies for recall. With procedures, a student might be able to perform the skill accurately and fluently in isolation, but have difficulty with the rules for when to apply the skill. Again, instruction will look different for teaching a new skill, teaching performance of a skill to fluency, or teaching application of the rules for when to perform the skill. If we don't consider and verify these levels of mastery of the knowledge, the probability of aligning instruction to student need decreases.

To test the assumed cause of not using context to confirm or self-correct word recognition, Ms. Smedley wanted Hubert to read from different materials rather than grade-appropriate text. She used text at his instructional level in order to ensure that his accuracy should be about 95%. She then replaced some key words so that the meaning would be interrupted (she substituted *horse* for *house*, *bed* for *red*, and *choice* for *cheese*—it made for an interesting read). She had Hubert read the passage without timing to see how he approached the task and asked him some questions about the substitutions afterword (he caught most of them, but was left puzzled about using milk to make choices).

ACTION 2.4: SUMMARIZE RESULTS

If you used the F.AC.T.R. worksheet for each problem and each assumed cause, summarization is a straightforward task. The result of each sheet provides an explicit summary of the test to determine whether that assumed cause was verified. The results across the F.AC.T.R. sheets are what should be summarized here.

With multiple problems and assumed causes, it is important to remember the priorities we set when generating them. Are the problems or causes still prioritized the same way, or does the new information suggest something is more or less important than we thought? When generating assumed causes, priority was given to skills that serve as prerequisites to other skills (i.e., ones that fall earlier in the skill sequence or standards). When considering priorities at this point, it is also important to think about nonverified assumed causes and the magnitude of problems.

If some assumed causes were not verified, it may be important to determine why they were not verified. An assumed cause might not have been verified because it was an incorrect assumption. This might happen if the assumed cause was generated from a source that was not accurate, either because it has poor reliability or validity or was not implemented with high fidelity. It could also happen if there was a misalignment of the assessment procedure used to verify the assumed cause. If the procedure does not accurately represent the skill and the conditions, you can get an accurate result, but not for what you wanted to assess.

If the "test" of F.AC.T.R. indicates that the student has not mastered the skill (i.e., that the assumed cause was verified), we also need to consider how close the student might be to mastering it. A student whose accuracy at the skill is expected to be 95% or greater who can consistently perform the skill at 90% accuracy is likely closer to mastering that skill than a student who consistently performs the skill at 20% accuracy.

When summarizing assessment results to verify assumed causes, it is important to remember to focus only on the relevant results. The assessment procedures were selected to be very closely aligned with the purpose, and therefore the results should also be aligned. However, some of the procedures for collecting the information in Action 2.3 yield a lot of other potential information. This can make it confusing to filter out the extra information in order to stick to what you need. For example, if you were using a miscue analysis of a student's reading of a passage to test assumed causes about his decoding or word recognition skills, there will be a lot of "noise" (i.e., extraneous information). If the student makes enough errors to be able to make sound decisions, there are likely to be errors that confirm the assumed cause and others that don't, either because they do not test the appropriate skill or they provide inconsistent results. In addition, because the student is performing this skill in context, he might be making that error for a reason other than the one we hypothesized (when reading, students make errors of decoding, semantics, syntax, attention, and more, but it is impossible to tell since they are just "errors").

This is one reason why it is useful to use the F.AC.T.R. sheet—it will keep your decision making focused on the decision you need to make provided you selected an appropriate assessment procedure.

When multiple assumed causes have been verified, all are important to consider, but the priority still needs to be set. Provided they are in a logical sequence, the most important is generally the one that falls earliest in the sequence. This is because it will serve as a prerequisite or tool skill for the others. If they do not fall in a logical sequence, a determination needs to be made about which ones might serve as prerequisites to others. For example, Hubert might have difficulty decoding prefixes and suffixes and also difficulty understanding the meaning of different prefixes and suffixes. Although both are skills to be mastered in his grade-level standards, Ms. Smedley decides that she wants to emphasize decoding the prefixes and suffixes before introducing their meaning, because if Hubert can't differentiate them from one another, he is less likely to be able to associate them with their meaning. His performance on the prefix and suffix list that she created indicated that he did confuse *pre-*, *re-*, and *de-* when reading.

QUESTION 2: WERE THE ASSUMED CAUSES VERIFIED?

Here we are again at an answering part. As we mentioned earlier, the questions at the end of each phase serve as a type of accuracy check. If you go through all four actions of the phase, but can't answer the question affirmatively, then you can't move on to the next phase. For Phase 2, if you weren't able to verify an assumed cause, there is no point in moving on to Phase 3 and planning and implementing instruction because that instruction should be designed to address the assumed cause that was verified in Phase 2. No verified assumed cause, no identified student need, nothing to align instruction with.

If the generation of assumed causes yielded only one, everything else was straightforward through Phase 2. However, there are often multiple potential assumed causes. If you generated multiple assumed causes or had multiple problems to address, this will be a multipart answer. It is always possible that some assumed causes are verified and others are not. As discussed for *Action 2.4*, it was important to consider why some were verified and some weren't to prioritize the needs that will be the basis of the intervention. The answers to this question are in relation to whether we were able to verify at least one assumed cause that can be used as the foundation for instruction planning.

No

If we were not able to verify a single assumed cause, we need to go back to the drawing board to generate and verify one (or more).

Yes

If we are able to verify the cause(s) of the problem, then it is time to move from Phase 2: Summative Decision Making to Phase 3: Formative Decision Making so that we can design and implement the intervention that will solve the problem we have identified.

CHAPTER SUMMARY

In this chapter, we presented the second phase of the CBE process. Phase 1: Fact Finding was about setting the stage for the detailed thinking required for Phase 2: Summative Decision Making as well as Phase 3: Formative Decision Making. In Phase 2, the confirmed problem was the basis of generating hypotheses about what is causing the problem. This process of determining what is causing the problem becomes the foundation for the next phase, as we move from verifying the cause to developing and implementing a solution.

CHAPTER 6

CBE Process Phase 3

Formative Decision Making

This chapter provides a detailed description of Phase 3 of the CBE process (see Figure 6.1). We conceptualize this phase as formative decision making to align with current thinking on different purposes of assessment and decision making. This is an iterative process wherein the educator is designing, implementing, and evaluating instruction or interventions provided to the student.

Formative decision making hinges on doing something different with the student from what was done in the past as well as monitoring student performance to determine whether the intervention is effective. To highlight the process we often use reading or math as the backdrop to explain each action within Phase 3. However, this process is not restricted to these content areas and can be applied to any area in which the student is having difficulty, including behavior.

We begin with the question that finished our summative decision making, "Were the assumed causes verified?" Once the answer is an emphatic "yes" (or at least a relatively confident "yes") formative decision making begins in earnest. The focus of Phase 3 is to ensure that we have picked an appropriate goal, the correct skill(s) to teach, and identified solutions to the problem and the details needed to carry them out. This starts by having a clear goal for the student and encompasses content to be taught, how it will be taught, and how students' progress will be monitored.

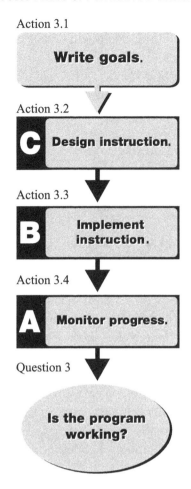

FIGURE 6.1. Phase 3 of the CBE process of inquiry: Formative decision making.

ACTION 3.1: WRITE GOALS

The term *goal* is another one that is used in many different ways in education. Goals can be long term, short term, end of year; we sometimes call them *objectives, learning targets,* or outcomes. The word *goal* might also make people think about IEPs, but this is not what we are referring to here (although it could be used for this purpose). We are using the term more broadly, referring to desired performance in reference to current performance.

When determining the goal for our student we can use components that will help us write a clearly understood goal. A goal that is articulated clearly provides us with a way to observe and measure student success. We use seven components when we write our goals.

1. *Time* (the amount of time the goal is written for)
    • "In 20 weeks . . . "
2. *Learner* (the student for whom the goal is being written)
    • " . . . Hubert will . . . "

3. *Behavior* (the specific skill the student will demonstrate)
   - " . . . read aloud . . . "
4. *Level* (the grade the content is from)
   - " . . . second-grade . . . "
5. *Content* (what the student is learning about)
   - " . . . reading . . . "
6. *Material* (what the student is using)
   - " . . . passage from OPR CBM progress monitoring material . . . "
7. *Criteria/CAP* (the expected level of performance including time and accuracy)
   - " . . . 90 words correctly in 1 minute with greater than 95% accuracy."

An example of a reading goal would be: In 20 weeks, Hubert will read aloud a second-grade reading passage from CBM progress monitoring material at 90 words correctly in 1 minute with greater than 95% accuracy.

The CAP is the desired performance we are shooting for. You might be asking yourself, "Self, where would I get these criteria?" We advocate for using a benchmark, or cut score, that has been predetermined by the test developer. The reason is that the benchmark (i.e., goal) is the level of performance a student needs to be able to achieve to have a high likelihood of success (i.e., meeting a criterion for proficiency) on a meaningful end-of-year assessment. Many progress monitoring instruments are also used for universal screening, which means you can use the end-of-year benchmark score on the universal screener for the goal of progress monitoring. If you currently use a universal screening instrument that does not have cut scores, there are alternate approaches for determining an appropriate goal (see Chapter 8 of *The ABCs of CBM* [Hosp et al., 2007] for a detailed discussion). For behavior goals, we encourage you to focus on increasing a positive behavior versus setting a goal for eliminating a negative behavior, but use similar standards and approaches for goal setting.

Having a clearly defined goal allows us to determine the difference between what our student can currently do and what it is we want him to be able to do. Knowing what we want him to be able to do helps us plan our instruction while considering the resources and amount of time we have with our student. Often the student needs instruction or practice with a prerequisite skill in order to master the skill included in the goal. It is important to keep in mind how prerequisite skills fit within the sequence of skills outlined in the CCSS. If you refer back to the example with Hubert from Chapter 5, being able to decode words with common prefixes and suffixes is important not only for second grade, but in third grade (and beyond). Understanding the goal for the student as well as the prerequisite skills he will need to get there informs our decisions around the instruction, which occurs in Action 3.2.

ACTION 3.2: DESIGN INSTRUCTION

The instruction should focus on those attributes of teaching we know are within the teacher's control and have a large impact on student learning. These details are represented in the visual shown in Figure 6.2, which illustrates the three F's (i.e., ***Frequency, Focus,*** and ***Format***) and one S (i.e., ***Size***) of instruction or intervention design. The center of the flower represents the intervention, and the flowerpot itself is the professional development needed to enact an intervention and the data needed to determine what the intervention is. We will start with the pot and work our way up to the flower.

In CBE, the pot is the professional development needed to train educators on the standards (e.g., reading, math, science, behavior) as well as specific educator skills such as assessing and instructing. Professional development is the sum

> **CBE MAXIM #13:**
>
> **Students with the greatest need need the greatest teaching!**

of instruction and support that we as educators receive. Although not a focus of this book, it is the reason we suggested making sure you are familiar with certain things including the foundations of CBE way back in Chapters 1 and 2. Good professional development provides the basis for determining what data to collect.

The data in the figure are represented by the soil from which the intervention grows. In this way, you can think of Phase 1: Fact Finding as the time to shovel all of our data into a pile to work with. Then Phase 2: Summative Decision Making becomes the time to roll up your sleeves, dig deep into the data, and get your hands dirty. From this work comes Phase 3: Formative Decision Making. Once we have confirmed the presence of the problem, verified the assumed cause(s), and identified the standard(s) that will serve as the goal, we move up the flower to the petals—three *F*'s and one S. These encompass things that we can influence to ensure we make a positive impact on student learning.

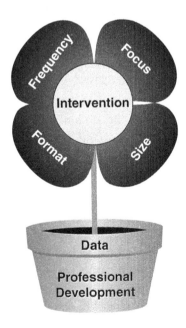

FIGURE 6.2. The "flower" of intervention design. From Florida Center for Reading Research (FCRR)/Just Read, Florida! and Florida Department of Education. Original image created by Elizabeth Crawford, Joseph Torgesen, and Christopher Bice.

Frequency

The first *F* covers how often instruction occurs: how many minutes each day, and how many days or weeks it will last. When working with a student who is struggling, most interventions require a 20- to 50-minute block for each session (Wanzek & Vaughn, 2008). This information is helpful and should be considered when setting up instructional schedules for the year. In addition to the number of minutes each day an intervention requires, is the number of weeks or duration that intervention is to be implemented. The number of weeks can vary greatly from 8 weeks up to 30 weeks (Torgesen et al., 2001; Vaughn, Linan-Thompson, & Hickman, 2003). If the number of weeks is short, then the number of minutes per day is usually increased. Looked at in this way, a teacher can block out her schedule to determine how many minutes per day are reasonable and over how many weeks. While these considerations are constrained by schedules, the needs of the student should drive how the intervention is set up. If the skills taught are prerequisites to other skills (and they probably are, because that is why they are essential and in the sequence or standards) on which all other learning hinges, then it is important to allow for the maximum number of minutes per day, but spend fewer weeks providing the intervention. Because the number of minutes per day and the number of weeks can both be adjusted, they should be planned for at the start of the school year. This allows us to build in schedules with the expectation that some students will need more.

Focus

The focus is in reference to the intervention or instruction. This can be defined broadly at first, such as one of the five major components of reading (i.e., phonemic awareness, phonics, fluency, comprehension, and vocabulary) but quickly needs to be narrowed down to look at specific skills within the broad category. This is why we develop and verify the assumed causes—the F.AC.T.R. process helps us to focus.

Having a good understanding of the CCSS can assist with what specific skills the student needs to learn and teachers should teach. A word of caution when defining the skills to teach is that if the focus is too broad, the student may not receive the specific instruction needed to improve his skills. On the other hand, if the skill is too narrow, then it might not lead to improvement within the broader skill. This is a fine balance between identifying the area of need and then narrowing that down to specific skills for instruction. Keep in mind that skills taught in isolation often do not transfer to broader understanding and generalization that is required to master a content area. For example, if the student needs instruction in phonics and we only provide instruction using words in isolation, he may not know how to transfer the skill to other situations such as reading those words within a passage. If, however, we teach phonics using isolated words and books that represent the same words, as well as writing the words in spelling and written assignments, then it is more likely he will not only learn phonics but also use this skill across tasks.

Format

The format includes specific details of how the instruction is delivered, which is the crux of Action 3.3 below.

Size

The number of students included within an instructional group is important. We know that smaller group sizes (around three) generally yield better outcomes than larger group sizes (around 10). In addition, there does not appear to be added benefit of one-on-one over small group (Elbaum, Vaughn, Hughes, & Moody, 1999; Vaughn et al., 2003). Therefore, the ideal intervention includes small groups of about three students, meets for 20 to 50 minutes per day, and is delivered for at least 8 weeks to see positive gains in student achievement. However, this doesn't mean that every intervention should look exactly like this.

The Heart of the Flower Is the Intervention

When you put everything together, it makes up the intervention. By changing elements that will have a large impact on student learning, we can focus on one factor at a time and determine how best to meet the needs of our students. It is important to note that some interventions have a higher likelihood of improving student learning. One way this is measured is by looking at the *effect size* an intervention produces when implemented with fidelity. There are resources and websites that provide this information for educators. These include the National Center for Intensive Interventions, the What Works Clearinghouse, the Center on Instruction, and many others (see the Resources section for more details). These sites allow you to search for interventions by elementary and secondary as well as subject areas such as math, reading, writing, and behavior. It is important to choose an intervention that has evidence to support its use for your particular purpose.

One last point about designing instruction before moving on to implementing it is the pacing. If a student is already behind, we need to pick up the pace as much as possible. This means that once a student has demonstrated knowledge of the

> **CBE MAXIM #14:**
>
> **Interventions are evidence based for specific purposes!**

skill, we need to get him practicing it often while we move on to instructing the next skill. Pacing often lags as the student and teacher experience success with teaching and learning a skill because it is reinforcing to continue doing something that you already know how to do. The student feels smart (as he should) that he learned and can perform the skill. You, the teacher, feel good (as you should) that you accomplished something and witnessed the student demonstrating a skill you taught. However, there must be a sense of urgency to keep working toward the goal. By lingering on skills the student has already learned, we waste valuable learning time.

So you might be asking yourself, "How do I know whether a student has already learned the skill and it is time to move on?" One sign to look for when you start the lesson is that the student can easily finish your words for you. When you

> **CBE MAXIM #15:**
>
> **The cure for slow learning is to teach faster!**

give the student additional practice materials and he grabs them like it's his favorite piece of candy and happily sits down to do it, it's time to move on. When you give him a pretest and he gets 100% correct, it's time to move on. Inherent in this is the point of making sure that we have identified that sweet spot (i.e., the zone of proximal development) so that we are always pushing the student to learn without being too far ahead into the land of complete frustration, but also without hanging back in the land of mastery, where he already knows the material. Somewhere in between mastery and frustration lives the best place for learning, because the student has mastered enough prerequisite skills to enable learning the new skill without having it be so far out of reach that success never comes. This truly is the art of teaching because this requires constant changing of instruction to keep the student within that sweet spot.

ACTION 3.3: IMPLEMENT INSTRUCTION

If the instruction was designed using all the components in Action 3.2, Action 3.3 is just the matter of using an appropriate format to teach it. This can be boiled down to *how* instruction is actually delivered, or the third *F* on the flower. A framework of seven steps provides the effective format features of instructional practices regardless of the focus of what we teach when implemented in order.

- *Step 1*: Present a clear goal/objective for each lesson.
              (e.g., "Today we will learn . . . ")
- *Step 2*: Give a reason for the importance of learning the skill.
              (e.g., "This will help you . . . ")
- *Step 3*: Show/demonstrate the skill and the criterion of acceptable performance.
              (e.g., "Watch me . . . "; "I do . . . ")
- *Step 4*: Practice the skill with the student.
              (e.g., "Let's do it together . . . "; "We do . . . ")
- *Step 5*: Observe the student performing the skill.
              (e.g., "Now you try . . . "; "You do . . . ")
- *Step 6*: Provide immediate and explicit feedback about the performance.
              (e.g., for a correct response: "That's correct"; for an incorrect response: "Watch me . . . "; "Now you try . . . ")
- *Step 7*: Additional practice of the skill.
              (e.g., "Let's do that again with . . . ")

If you notice, each step starts with an action the teacher does and includes example statements of how to start this step. This requires planning as well as building a routine. Each step is discussed in more detail below.

Step 1: Present a Clear Goal/Objective for Each Lesson

This step requires an understanding of what skills we teach and how that fits within the larger scope of skills (i.e., the standards) we want all students to learn. In order to tell students what they will learn explicitly, planning must occur ahead of time. This assists us as well as the student. We have to justify why we are spending time teaching the skill and link it to the objectives already identified. If we can't justify why the skill is to be taught, it might not be the right skill. Being able to clearly articulate what the lesson is about should maximize teaching time, as it provides a clear purpose, which also makes it easier to stay on topic.

Our student also benefits by hearing what he will be learning because it gives him a reason to attend to the lesson. Understanding the purpose and content of the lesson allows our student to focus his attention on learning. While it may be appropriate to assume adults understand why certain skills need to be taught, retaught, practiced, and mastered, it is not always obvious for the learner—particularly our student who is struggling in school. It also gives him direction and control over his learning in that he has a purpose if he can understand why he is asked to perform certain skills. The old "Because I said so" is not helpful to support learning.

Step 2: Give a Reason for the Importance of Learning the Skill

Taking it one step further, we should share not just what we want Hubert to learn, but why he needs to learn the skill. This step benefits Hubert and us. As with Step 1, we have to plan ahead in order to make the connection of "why" he needs to learn this skill. It goes beyond "Because it is in the CCSS," or "Because it is in our textbooks" (more detailed versions of "because I said so"). It is more about how learning a particular skill will benefit him now and in the future as he learns and masters new skills. Giving a reason for "why" places the importance on a skill within the bigger picture of mastering content and using the skill in years to come. This sounds easy, but it does take practice. For example, it is easy to explain why knowing how to decode words with common prefixes and suffixes is necessary and will be used throughout one's life. This information can be shared with the student by saying:

> "Knowing prefixes and suffixes will help you by knowing how to consistently read certain chunks of a word that are always pronounced the same way. It will also help you understand what the word means. So it will help with your decoding and vocabulary whenever you read."

The benefit of Step 2 is making the connection between what is learned and why it matters. This step is too often neglected in teaching as a lot of time is spent "doing stuff" with our students without them knowing what it is all for. The discussion of why it is important for our student to learn certain skills is also helpful when meeting with his parents. It provides a clear roadmap for us to share with Hubert and his parents that goes a long way toward building a

CBE MAXIM #16:
There is no "me" in learning!

team that works together in his best interest. Imagine sitting down with his parents and being able to tell them that Hubert has learned many of the basic reading skills needed to read words in text, but that he still needs to work on reading words that have certain prefixes and suffixes. You could even share which prefixes and suffixes you are working on and explain that it is important for Hubert to learn them so that when he encounters them with any printed material he will be able to read them and focus on the meaning of what he is reading.

Step 3: Show/Demonstrate the Skill and the Criterion of Acceptable Performance

Having a clear model of what the behavior looks like when performed correctly will increase the chances of our student doing what is expected. We call this the "I do" portion of the lesson. It is also the positive example of what the behavior looks like. Having clear criteria of what he needs to be able to do in order for us to determine whether he has it is critical for learning and maximizing instructional time. As with Steps 1 and 2, it does require pre-planning. However, if we have already conducted Steps 1 and 2, Step 3 should not be a far stretch. We need a clear understanding of what it would look like in order to determine that our student is learning the skill.

Having a model of what the skill looks like when performed correctly also allows us to compare our student's current performance to the model of expected performance. This information is used to guide changes to instruction that need to occur. For example, if the criterion is to read 12 different prefixes and suffixes with 100% accuracy, we set the expected performance against which the student's current performance is consistently measured. The student benefits from having a clear model of acceptable performance as he gets to see what it looks like to perform the skill successfully. This increases the chances that he will attend to the task as well as learn the skill with fewer errors.

With behavior standards, this would include showing our student what it looks like to perform the behavior. For example, if the behavior is about greeting friends appropriately, we would show him what his body would be doing as well as what words he would use when greeting a friend appropriately. Sometimes our student needs to "see it" in order to understand exactly what is being asked of him. This also provides a clear reference point when providing him with feedback.

Step 4: Practice the Skill with the Student

This step provides the insurance that our student understands what we have asked him to do by observing him do it. We call this the "We do" portion of the lesson. This is where our student or students respond in unison (or perform the skill) along with us. This provides us with evidence that what we did in Steps 1–3 was clear and understood by our students. We would not move on to the next skill if it was evident that our student did not yet understand what he is expected to do. Once it is clear, and our student understands what to do, we can move onto the next step.

Step 5: Observe the Student Performing the Skill

This is the "You do" part of the lesson. Our student responds or performs the behavior on his own. Without asking him to perform the task individually, we would not know whether he needed additional assistance or whether he was ready to move on to the next skill. This step provides a direct observation to compare the desired level of performance to his current level of performance.

Our student benefits from this step by having to demonstrate his understanding of the task. Having a clear model of acceptable performance along with the requirement of demonstrating the skill increases his chances of learning the skill correctly the first time by not allowing him to practice the incorrect response. However, if he makes an error, we quickly move on to the next step and provide immediate feedback.

Step 6: Provide Immediate and Explicit Feedback about the Performance

This step requires us to have a correction response planned ahead of time. If our student's performance is correct, we praise or congratulate him and move on to the next step, which requires him to practice or demonstrate the skill independently. However, if he doesn't provide the correct response, we should provide immediate corrective feedback to minimize time spent doing the wrong thing and maximize time spent doing the correct thing. The old saying "practice makes perfect" only works if what you are practicing is correct. It is more accurate to say "perfect practice makes perfect" (thank you, Coach Dalton).

We need to think about the easiest way to remodel the correct response but also come up with additional models to share with the student. The first logical step would be to repeat Step 3 and have our student watch what is expected of him. Then Step 4 would be repeated to see whether he does it correctly. If our student is successful with this additional modeling, we move on to Step 6. However, if he is still not able to perform the skill, then how we demonstrate the skill needs to change. For example, if we ask Hubert to say the sound for *z* but instead he gives the sound for *s*, we could expand the model by having him put his hand to his throat and feel the vibration when he says /z/ versus no vibration when he says /s/. We need to decide whether Hubert needs further instruction or lacks a prerequisite skill in order to be able to perform the skill. This will determine the needed level of instruction and next steps. The first place to start would be to (1) repeat Steps 3 and 4, (2) provide additional instruction, or (3) teach a prerequisite skill. Once Hubert has learned the skill, we can move on to Step 7.

Step 7: Additional Practice of the Skill

This step requires us to plan for additional learning opportunities and practice for our student to learn the skill. This can include additional time to practice the same skill with similar and/or different material. As with each of these steps, planning what these opportunities and materials are ahead of time is a requirement. It is also important for our student to practice the skill within a larger context of how he would be using it. For example, if Hubert is practicing decoding prefixes and suffixes it is important that he learns these in isolation, attached to words, and within text. If he cannot apply or transfer the skill to a larger skill set then he has not yet learned the skill to mastery. Learning skills in isolation can be helpful for initial acquisition, but ultimately it is not as beneficial as learning them across skill sets. The end goal should be having the student demonstrate the skill in the most meaningful way possible. In the example of decoding prefixes and suffixes, it would be in reading text. For behavior, it would include using that skill within its natural setting.

The student benefits from this step by demonstrating his knowledge of what he learned in meaningful ways. This is where the ownership of what is taught is transferred to what he has learned. Our student is now able to demonstrate his skills independent of instructional support and at a level that affects learning beyond knowing the skill in isolation. Critical to showing whether he has learned this skill is having a clear model against which to compare his performance (Step 3). This provides guidance for selecting the tools to monitor our student's learning in order to reach an established level of mastery (monitoring student progress is Action 3.4—stay tuned). Figures 6.3 and 6.4 provide examples of lesson formats for reading and behavior, respectively.

Consistent in each step is the necessity to preplan. While this may add time and require resources up front, these steps and materials will not need to change once they are developed, saving time in the future. Once we are familiar with this type of instructional focus or routine, the engagement and facilitation of student learning increases. This makes the jobs of teaching and learning much more rewarding experiences. Also rewarding is seeing student improvement on a progress monitoring assessment.

Step 1: Present a clear goal/objective for each lesson.
"Today we are going to learn how to read and spell words with the sound /oi/, like *foil* and *boy*. We know that /oi/ is spelled *oi* when it is in the middle of a word like *foil* and *oy* when it is at the end of a word like *boy*."
Step 2: Give a reason for why leaning the skill is important.
"There are many words with this sound, and learning how to read and spell them will make it easier for you when you see and spell words with the /oi/ sound."
Step 3: Show/demonstrate the skill and the criterion of acceptable performance.
"Watch me and listen for the /oi/ sound: *foil, join, noise, point, boy, ahoy, convoy, destroy*."
Step 4: Practice the skill with the student.
"Now let's read them together: *foil, join, noise, point, boy, ahoy, convoy, destroy*."
Step 5: Observe the student performing the skill.
"Now it's your turn to read them: *foil, join, noise, point, boy, ahoy, convoy, destroy*."
Step 6: Provide immediate and explicit feedback about the performance.
[Student reads *join* as "jon."] "Stop. That word is *join*. Now you say it." [Student responds by reading "join."]
Step 7: Additional practice of the skill.
"Now I want you to practice reading some more words with the /oi/ sound in them. Then you will read this text which has many /oi/ words in it so you can practice this skill in stories."

FIGURE 6.3. Example of a reading lesson using the seven steps to implement instruction.

Step 1: Present a clear goal/objective for each lesson.
"Today we are going to learn how to enter the classroom appropriately, keeping our bodies to ourselves and with quiet voices."
Step 2: Give a reason for why learning the skill is important.
"When many people are working within a small space, we need to know how to come and go without disrupting others."
Step 3: Show/demonstrate the skill and the criterion of acceptable performance.
"Watch me as I enter the room and move to my seat, keeping my body to myself and my voice low."
Step 4: Practice the skill with the student.
"Now let's all enter the room together keeping our bodies to ourselves and our voices low."
Step 5: Observe the student performing the skill.
"Now it's your turn to enter the room and I will watch."
Step 6: Provide immediate and explicit feedback about the performance.
[Student bumps into another student as they enter the room.] "Stop. Your body entered another person's space. See how I leave room all around me so I can move without bumping into people. Now you try it." [Student responds by reentering room without bumping into anyone.]
Step 7: Additional practice of the skill.
"Now I want you to practice every time you enter into a room by making sure you are keeping your body to yourself and using a low voice. We will practice this every time we come and go from our room today."

FIGURE 6.4. Example of a behavior lesson using the seven steps to implement instruction.

ACTION 3.4: MONITOR PROGRESS

Monitoring student progress is used to *inform* teachers; hence this is the last action under Phase 3 on formative decision making. The power of progress monitoring is that it provides a technically sound way to index student academic growth across time (Deno, 1985; Fuchs & Deno, 1991). The same principles apply to monitoring progress related to behaviors. The ability to monitor student growth gets at the heart of the question, "Is the student improving given the instruction we are providing?" Without being able to answer this question, we don't know whether the interventions we are delivering are helping the student improve. In order to determine whether the student is improving, we need to identify the progress monitoring instrument that will help us measure the goal we have identified in Action 3.1. In order to choose a progress monitoring instrument we need to consider at least four criteria. It must:

1. Have enough equivalent forms so that it can be used over time and the student will not be able to memorize any of the material *or* repeatable in that it measures the same way each time (useful with behavior when using rating scales, checklists, or observations).

2. Be sensitive to student improvement, typically indicated by a coefficient for slope,

so that any change in the student's score is an accurate reflection of an increase in skill and not due to change in the measurement or instrument. For behavior, change in performance is a true indication of change and not drift in how it is recorded.

3. Be technically adequate (i.e., with good reliability and validity).

4. Measure something meaningful that is either directly tied to instruction (i.e., a mastery measure) or a slightly more distal measure (i.e., a general outcome measure) that can be affected as a result of instruction.

Additional considerations for observations (which are typically how behavior is monitored) include making sure the desired behavior is measured consistently. Because observations rely on someone's judgment, they are more vulnerable to *measurement drift* (i.e., not recording or applying decision criteria consistently over time). A clear articulation of what the behavior looks like will help increase the reliability of how it is measured.

Choosing Progress Monitoring Instruments

Given the four criteria necessary for an instrument to be useful to monitor progress you might be asking yourself, "So what progress monitoring instruments are available to me?" and, "How do I choose the right one?"[1] In part due to research on effective practices as well as its inclusion in federal and state requirements, there has been an increased interest in progress monitoring. The National Center on Progress Monitoring, the Research Institute on Progress Monitoring, the National Center on Response to Intervention, and the National Center on Intensive Interventions have been proactive in seeking out progress monitoring materials and conducting reviews so that consumers have access to "tool charts" to compare and select progress monitoring instruments (think *Consumer Reports* for assessment instruments). The National Center on Intensive Interventions continues to provide reviews of progress monitoring instruments. The tool chart can be sorted by grade level (elementary or middle school) and by subject (reading, math, and writing). This is a valuable resource for educators and a good starting place to identify progress monitoring instruments for academic skills. Because lists of progress monitoring instruments can be found at the National Center on Intensive Intervention and elsewhere (Hosp et al., 2007) we won't provide a list here. However, it's important to discuss the difference between mastery measures and general outcome measures because it affects which type of instrument you will want to use.

The best place to start making the distinction between mastery measures or general outcome measures is to understand the purpose of each and how they are similar and different from each other. The purpose of mastery measures is to collect student data that are skill specific like a sheet with single-digit addition problems or high-frequency words. Mastery measures (MMs) are extremely helpful when the focus of instruction is on a narrow skill or set of skills and we need to make a decision about that skill. When used to moni-

---

[1] As in the rest of this book, we focus primarily on academic skills. For monitoring behavior we refer you to *School-Based Behavioral Assessment: Informing Intervention and Instruction* (Chafouleas, Riley-Tillman, & Sugai, 2007) or *Daily Behavior Report Cards: An Evidence-Based System of Assessment and Intervention* (Volpe & Fabiano, 2013).

tor progress, they help answer the question "Is the student learning how to perform this discrete skill more accurately and fluently?" This has direct and immediate implications for what we teach and how we teach it depending on how the student performs on the progress monitoring MM.

The purpose of general outcome measures (GOMs) is to collect student data that are broader and an indicator of overall performance in an area. For example, a sheet of math problems that includes multiple skills such as addition, subtraction, multiplication, and division, or reading a passage of text would be GOMs that require the student to perform a more general skill (mixed-math computation or oral reading). GOMs are helpful because they focus across an entire year or grade level. They help answer the questions: "Is the student learning the math skills we would expect him to know by the end of second grade?" or "Is the student learning how to read text fluently at his grade level?" Similar to MMs, GOMs also have direct and immediate implications for what we teach and how we teach it. The difference is that MMs help identify specific skills while GOMs indicate when instruction may need to change.

Both types of instrument should be administered in the same standardized way. This is why CBE relies heavily on CBM. CBMs are short in duration (1–5 minutes), use standardized procedures for administration and scoring, and provide a score of accuracy and fluency of skills. Other similarities are that data from both can be graphed and compared to the goal and progress toward that goal identified in Action 3.1.

The differences between MMs and GOMs include how well they gauge student learning relative to specific skills or more general skills. For example, a MM measuring high-frequency words loses the bigger picture of having the student read high-frequency words within text that would be captured using a GOM such as OPR. Related to this, MMs do not provide information about retention or generalization while GOMs do. With MMs, the instruments and tasks are always changing, which makes it impossible to gauge whether the student has retained previously mastered skills and is able to generalize to new skills across the content area.

Based on this, you may want to use a MM along with a GOM to monitor student progress. The MM provides information about whether the student is learning the specific skill that is the focus of instruction, while the GOM provides information about whether the student is making progress toward the broader goal. Spending some time thinking about what you want the student to learn and looking at Table 6.1, which lists attributes of each type of progress monitoring instrument, should help you decide which to use for what purpose.

Frequency of Monitoring

Once you decide which progress monitoring instrument to use, you will need to determine how often to use it. One rule of thumb is that the greater the discrepancy between the student's performance and the expected performance, the more often you should measure his skills (i.e., monitor his progress). Most progress monitoring instruments are designed to be used on a weekly basis. For behavior, you may want to increase this to daily or even throughout the day. The same rule applies that the more discrepant the current behavior is

TABLE 6.1. Attributes of Mastery Measures and General Outcome Measures for Academic Skills

Positive attributes	Mastery measures	General outcome measures
Administration and scoring is short in duration (1–5 minutes).	✓	✓
Standardized accuracy and scoring procedures.	✓	✓
Represents accuracy and fluency of skill.	✓	✓
Data are applicable for graphing.	✓	✓
Aligned to specific skills.	✓	
Aligned to broad skills.		✓
Measures generalization.		✓
Measures retention.		✓
Represents end-of-year competencies.		✓
Informs instruction for specific skills.	✓	

from the expected behavior, the more frequently progress should be monitored. The other factor is the importance attached to the skill. Some academic and social skills are so foundational that unless students have mastered them they will not make adequate progress in the broader skill area. For example, in reading a student must be able to decode unfamiliar words in order to focus on comprehension, the broader goal of reading. Therefore, decoding is so foundational that unless students can do this they will not become accomplished readers. For behavior, if a student cannot focus his attention long enough to learn the content, then attention is so foundational that unless the student can do this he will not become accomplished in any social and/or academic area.

Graphing Student Performance

Another important component of progress monitoring is graphing the results. When graphing student data, it is just as critical to capture correct responses as it is to capture incorrect responses (i.e., student errors). Graphing and tracking errors are critical because for a student to become proficient in a skill he needs to perform it at a certain level of ***automaticity***, a combination of accuracy and rate.

It is often argued that you cannot be proficient in anything unless you meet criteria for both rate (how many correct responses within a time period) and accuracy (the percentage of correct responses). You can get four different combinations of accuracy and rate, but only one equals proficiency.

1. Accurate + Slow = Not Proficient
2. Inaccurate + Fast = Not Proficient
3. Inaccurate + Slow = Not Proficient
4. Accurate + Fast = Proficient

The other point to make is that just because a student is making progress does not mean you should stop monitoring progress or even reduce how often you monitor progress. Until the student has met the goal, for both accuracy and rate, his progress should be monitored by charting and/or graphing his scores.

Having our student's data graphed allows us to make some quick decisions about his progress. However, this is only true if we are graphing the data appropriately. You might think that a graph is a graph is a graph (or that the graph is always greener). However, what type of graph is used or how the data are graphed can affect the decisions we make. The Y axis (i.e., vertical) should represent the metric that you are measuring. For example, in reading, it could be the number of words read correctly per minute on a passage along with errors. For math, it could be the number of digits computed correctly along with errors on a mixed-math sheet. For behavior, this would be the number of times the student performs the correct behavior. The X axis (i.e., horizontal) should always represent the number of days or weeks the student will be monitored. This allows you to plan ahead—you can show how many days or weeks an intervention will be provided right on the graph along with what skills you will be measuring.

The range of scores affects how the data look. Looking at the two graphs in Figure 6.5, you might conclude that the top graph represents better growth than the bottom graph. However, they are the same data, just represented with different ranges applied to the Y axis.

You can see for yourself that it can be confusing when different scales are used, so we recommend standardizing the scales on graphs for each skill you would monitor. This provides a set of graphs that can then be used with other classrooms or students. It can be useful when making comparisons between different students, classrooms, interventions, or any other difference you might want to compare. For example, if a particular intervention is being used by three different teachers with five different students, someone might ask, "How are the students performing who are getting the Super Duper Intervention for Reading?"[2] By using the same instruments and graphs, this information is easily obtained by either (1) putting the graphs side by side and making comparisons, or (2) putting all of the students onto one graph with each student represented by a different color to identify who is who. See Figure 6.6 for an example of what this might look like.

This is a good way to determine whether an intervention is working for a group of students as well as for any individual student. It also could be used to see which teachers

---

[2]Do not attempt to buy the Super Duper Intervention for Reading. It is a fictional program for illustrative purposes only.

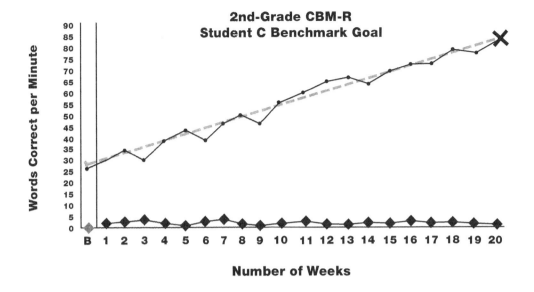

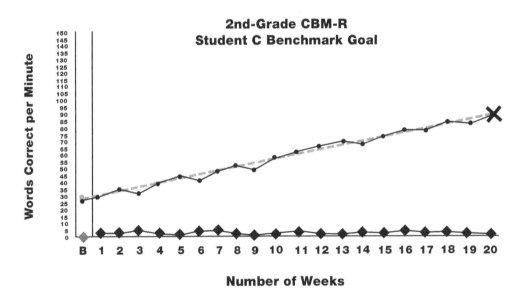

FIGURE 6.5. Graphs showing the effect of having the Y axis compressed or stretched out.

might be having more success with the intervention over other teachers. This could provide a great opportunity for teachers to share their successes and struggles around a particular intervention so that they can support and learn from each other.

Once you have determined what type of graph to use, you need some guidelines on how to interpret the information that is on the graph. Before you can make a judgment about how a student is progressing you need to have enough data. This ensures that there are enough data points available to make an informed decision and error associated with the assessment is not responsible for how the data look. A general rule is to collect at least

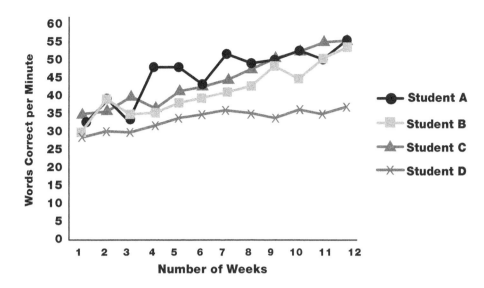

FIGURE 6.6. Progress monitoring graph with four students represented getting the same Super Duper Reading Intervention.

6 to 8 data points and then refer to the last 4 consecutive data points to make some decisions. Table 6.2 revisits the four different combinations of accuracy and rate and applies the 4-consecutive-data-points rule as well as providing guidance for next steps.

Using this table allows you to look at the last 4 consecutive data points along with the accuracy and rate data to determine what to do next. Another way data can be looked at is to graph a trend line and compare this line to the *goal line* (which connects the initial point, or baseline, with the goal). The *trend line* is the actual trajectory of the student's growth based on 7 to 8 data points. The graphs in Figure 6.7 provide examples of what these two different types of decisions would look like using the same data, but applying the 4-point

TABLE 6.2. Guidance for Using the 4-Point Decision Rule

Accuracy and rate combinations	Last 4 data points	Guidance for next steps
1. Accurate + Slow = Not Proficient	Below goal line	Keep instruction the same but increase practice and keep the same goal.
2. Inaccurate + Fast = Not Proficient	Above goal line	Investigate instruction and keep the same goal.
3. Inaccurate + Slow = Not Proficient	Below goal line	Investigate instruction, prerequisite skills, and keep the same goal.
4. Accurate + Fast = Proficient	Above goal line	Move on to the next skill to teach and raise the goal.

decision rule (the top graph) versus using a trend line (the bottom graph). You can see that both indicate something needs to change.

CBE MAXIM #17:

None of us teaches as well as all of us!

Once you have reviewed a student's graph you will make one of three decisions: (1) continue with the instruction, (2) change something about the instruction, or (3) move on to a new skill altogether. When a change in instruction is warranted, we want to be clear that we are *not* suggesting you throw out everything that you have used and start over. Often it is more appropriate to walk back through the CBE process to deter-

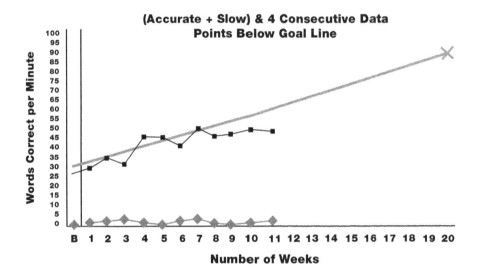

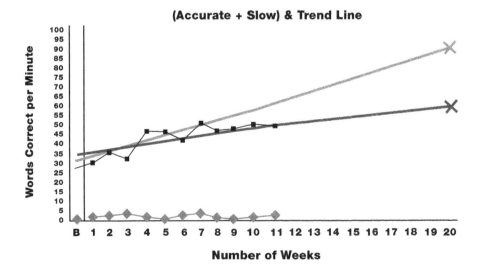

FIGURE 6.7. Looking at "Accurate + Slow" using the 4-point rule or a trend line.

mine what specifically needs to be changed or adjusted. It could be that the instructional program is working, but the student would benefit from more opportunities to engage with the instruction. In this case, increasing the frequency and duration of the instruction may be all that is required. Think back to the first *F* on the flower (Frequency). It is a lot easier to increase the amount of time a student engages with something than it is to start over.

Despite our best efforts, sometimes the student will not make the progress we expect and the data on the student's progress monitoring graph indicate that a change is warranted. When this happens, we turn to the final step in the CBE process—*troubleshooting*. The troubleshooting chapter will provide guidance as well as helpful checklists to use as you work your way backward through the CBE flowchart. This will allow you to pinpoint where the breakdown in the learning process might be occurring so that you can make the adjustments needed and get back to teaching.

CHAPTER SUMMARY

In this chapter, we presented the third phase of the CBE process in greater detail. This phase of formative decision making is really "where the rubber hits the road" for most educators. Because we are focused on solving learning problems that are complex, it is crucial to be planful in our design of the instruction to solve the problem and diligent in our delivery of the instruction. Placing the cause of the student's learning problem in the context of prerequisite skills in the previous, present, and next grade standards, we can develop a clear plan not only for the current instruction that needs to occur, but also for what needs to come next. By attending to the aspects of effective instruction, we increase the probability that the instruction will address the student's needs. By monitoring the student's progress, we have the path that learning will take toward that goal. However, even though we were extremely planful and attentive, sometimes students do not progress in ways we expect. When this is the case and the student does not learn what we need him to at the necessary rate, it is time to troubleshoot the CBE process to see where the process broke down and what we can do to fix it.

CHAPTER 7

Troubleshooting the CBE Process

This chapter provides a detailed description of each of the five steps involved in trouble-shooting. We conceptualized this part of CBE as the "HELP ME!!!" part. The need for help will be apparent if our student is *not* making sufficient progress as indicated on the progress monitoring assessment. After all of the hard work and time spent being planful and focused as we worked through the CBE process, we know what can happen to even the best-laid plans. We need to have a plan for when things start to go south, because, as we all know, things *will* go south.

Checkpoints A, B, C, D, and E in troubleshooting (see Figure 7.1) all correspond to something we have already done. We have organized the checkpoints so that we don't start from the beginning, but rather we work our way back through the actions and ask ourselves very specific questions to see whether we have missed something or have not followed through with something we assumed was happening. Our level of frustration can run high when we have worked diligently to identify our student's needs and attend to them with the best instructional strategies we have, only to realize his performance is not improving. Trouble-shooting therefore, stops us from going over the deep end by providing guidelines that will identify what we need to change instead of throwing it all away and starting over.

> **TROUBLESHOOTING TIP #1:**
>
> **Always start with the most obvious place, since it will be the easiest to fix.**

We have all experienced the frustration of doing our best, yet seeing little improvement for our student(s). What if we told you that you didn't need to pull your hair out anymore? Sound too good to be true? Well, we hope that the steps outlined in this chapter will do just that by providing some guidelines, checklists, and helpful tips to follow.

A common root of the problem is often fidelity of implementation; that is, how well we follow through and do what we are supposed to do. While it sounds easy, it is helpful to have

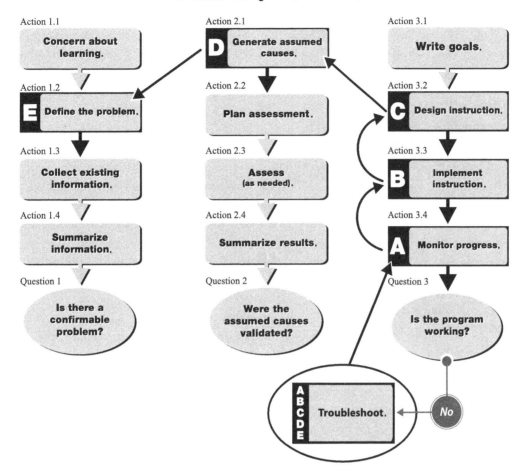

FIGURE 7.1. Flow of the checkpoints for troubleshooting CBE.

checklists and guides to keep us on the straight and narrow. In order to see improvement in student's skills, it is critical that we implement our instruction and monitor progress the way that it was designed, standardized, and validated. The absence of fidelity will lead to the absence of student improvement. We will start our investigation with Checkpoint A—Action 3.4 Monitor Progress.

> **TROUBLESHOOTING TIP #2:**
>
> **Lack of fidelity will lead to lack of student improvement.**

CHECKPOINT A—ACTION 3.4: MONITOR PROGRESS

If our student is not showing improvement on the progress monitoring graph, we need to ask ourselves some questions. The first is about the fidelity of how we have collected the data. There are specific things we can check off that should occur before, during, and after collecting progress monitoring data. By first reviewing how the data are collected, we may quickly find that it has everything to do with our actions and nothing to do with our student not learning the desired skills. By following Form 7.1 we can narrow down if fidelity of how we collect data is the problem.

> **TROUBLESHOOTING TIP #3:**
>
> **Use a countdown timer so that you can focus on the student and not have to watch the time.**

For example, if we realize Ms. Smedley is not consistently using a timer, we would figure this out under *Before*. What if we realize Ms. Smedley is not adhering to the exact time when she collects data? We would figure this out under *During*. What if we find out Ms. Smedley was not adding up the score correctly? We would identify this under *After*. Each of these checkpoints provides us with valuable information that is easy to fix, and all three are likely explanations for inaccurate data.

> **TROUBLESHOOTING TIP #4:**
>
> **Look at what is happening before, during, and after data are being collected.**

If we find out the data are collected with fidelity, we can congratulate Ms. Smedley and look at other features of data collection that might be problematic. The questions below provide us with some suggestions of where to look next:

- *Question 1*: Are the progress monitoring data graphed correctly?
- *Question 2*: Is the goal appropriate and is the goal line drawn?
- *Question 3*: Are data collected in a timely manner?
- *Question 4*: Is the right progress monitoring instrument being used?

Question 1: Are the Progress Monitoring Data Graphed Correctly?

We know the Y axis (vertical line) should represent the metric we are measuring and the X axis (horizontal line) should always represent the number of days or weeks we are monitoring progress. The range of scores on the Y axis is also critical, as it will compress or expand

> **TROUBLESHOOTING TIP #5:**
>
> **Always start the Y axis with 0 so accuracy/errors can be graphed along with correct responses.**

the look of the data. By following the checklist in Form 7.2 we can determine whether there is a problem with how we have graphed the data. If we have graphed the data correctly, we can move on to Question 2; if not, we can stop and fix it.

Question 2: Is the Goal Appropriate and Is the Goal Line Drawn?

> **TROUBLESHOOTING TIP #6:**
>
> **Use the benchmark score that represents the spring benchmark for the goal.**

To help determine whether we set the goal appropriately we can look up the end-of-year benchmark for the progress monitoring instrument we are using. These benchmarks correspond to the universal screening benchmarks associated with

Fidelity Checklist for before, during, and after Conducting Progress Monitoring

Before		
1. Has the correct student material and teacher/examiner material.	**YES**	**NO**
2. Has a pen/pencil to mark teacher/examiner sheet.	**YES**	**NO**
3. Has a countdown timer that shows seconds or a stopwatch.	**YES**	**NO**
4. Has a clipboard and holds it so the student cannot see the examiner's materials.	**YES**	**NO**
During		
5. Reads the standardized directions verbatim.	**YES**	**NO**
6. Starts the stopwatch according to the directions.	**YES**	**NO**
7. Follows the procedure for time allowed on each item.	**YES**	**NO**
8. Marks the student's errors on the teacher/examiner sheet.	**YES**	**NO**
9. Does not correct the student when he/she makes an error (except when allowed in the example material only).	**YES**	**NO**
10. Follows the discontinuation rule.	**YES**	**NO**
11. Administers the task for the correct amount of time.	**YES**	**NO**
12. Stops the student at the end of the time and marks where the student stops.	**YES**	**NO**
After		
13. Adds up the number of errors correctly.	**YES**	**NO**
14. Determines the total number of items attempted.	**YES**	**NO**
15. Scores the task by subtracting the errors from the total attempted.	**YES**	**NO**
16. Prorates the score if the student finishes the task before the time is up.	**YES**	**NO**

most progress monitoring instruments. If an end-of-year benchmark is not available, we can use norms. Once we confirm that the goal is correct, we need to make sure we drew the goal line correctly. To do this, we will look at the goal and determine whether we drew a line from the goal to the first data point on the graph. Once we determine we have done this correctly, we can move on to Question 3.

> **TROUBLESHOOTING TIP #7:**
>
> **The goal should represent a skill for that student's grade if at all possible.**

Question 3: Are Data Collected in a Timely Manner?

In order to determine whether our student is making gains with the instruction he is receiving, we need to collect data on a consistent basis over some predetermined set of weeks. Things we need to think about that will affect data collection are:

- Day of the week (pick one day and try to stick with it each week).
- Time of day (if we know the student is always late to school, then first thing in the morning is not going to work).
- Same person collects data each week (person providing instruction should also collect data).
- Data are collected *each* week.

It may seem silly to put time and energy into making a plan to collect data that takes into consideration all four points above. However, it will make a difference in how useful the information will be. If we are going to spend the time to collect progress monitoring data, then it only makes sense to try to stack the deck in our favor. We highly recommend that the person providing the intervention is the same person who collects the data. This provides the person who is delivering the instruction a firsthand look to see how the student is doing when he applies his skills.

We also recommend that if you miss a data collection point, you should try to collect it ASAP. If we normally collect data every Friday morning and our student does not show up until the afternoon, we can do one of two things. First, we can collect the data that same day but in the afternoon. Second, we can wait and collect it on Monday morning the next week. If we collect it on Monday morning the following week then we also need to collect again on Friday of the same week so that we have at least one data point for each week. We should never sit a student down, give him two or more progress monitoring instruments, and graph them as if they occurred across different weeks. This is a waste of our time as well as our student's time. It will provide us with a set of data that is not accurate and therefore not useful. If we are collecting the data appropriately then we will look at Question 4 next.

> **TROUBLESHOOTING TIP #8:**
>
> **Pick a time of day when the student performs best and keep that time consistent when collecting progress monitoring data.**

FORM 7.2

Checklist for Troubleshooting Action 3.4: Monitoring Progress

Directions: Read each question, then answer the follow-up questions with either YES or NO The first NO you circle, STOP, and go back and fix it.

Question 1: Are the progress monitoring data graphed correctly?	Does the *Y* axis represent the metric for the progress monitoring assessment? **YES** **NO**	Does the *X* axis represent the number of weeks for monitoring progress? **YES** **NO**
Question 2: Is the goal appropriate and is the goal line drawn?	Is the goal line set on an end-of-year benchmark for the assessments? **YES** **NO**	Is the goal line drawn from the first data point to the end-of-the-year benchmark? **YES** **NO**
Question 3: Are data collected in a timely manner?	Are data collected each week, on the same day, and at the same time of day? **YES** **NO**	Is it the same person each week who collects the data? **YES** **NO**
Question 4: Is the right progress monitoring assessment being used?	Does the progress monitoring assessment measure a skill or skill set associated with the instruction (e.g., alignment between instruction and assessment)? **YES** **NO**	Does the progress monitoring assessment have relevance for a student at this grade level (e.g., is the assessment grade appropriate)? **YES** **NO**

Question 4: Are the Right Progress Monitoring Instruments Being Used?

Suggestions for identifying whether we are using the right progress monitoring instrument starts with us examining whether the instrument we chose aligns with the skills we are teaching.

- Does the progress monitoring instrument measure a skill or skill set associated with the instruction (i.e., is there strong alignment between instruction and assessment)?
- Does the progress monitoring instrument have relevance for a student at this grade level (i.e., is the instrument grade appropriate)?

Let us tackle the first question, which asks how closely our instruction and assessment are aligned. If Hubert is receiving instruction on a specific decoding strategy, then we would want to use a progress monitoring instrument that is related to decoding. For example, nonsense words or OPR are two progress monitoring instruments that can be used and are related to decoding. Nonsense words is a MM because it is a purer measure of decoding. OPR is a GOM because it measures more than just decoding. However, students cannot read a passage unless they can decode words. Used in this way, OPR is a proxy for the skills associated with decoding. We would not want to use a letter naming task for progress monitoring because it is not related to decoding.

This brings us to the second question and the relevance for using a progress monitoring instrument that is closely aligned with our student's grade level. Sticking with the same example, we know that decoding can be measured using three common progress monitoring instruments: letter sounds, nonsense words, and OPR. Depending on the grade the student is in, we should pick the progress monitoring instrument that is closest to his grade. For example, we would want to use letter sounds if the student was in prekindergarten or kindergarten. If the student was in kindergarten or first grade, we would use nonsense words; and if the student was in first grade or beyond, we would use OPR. Once we identify the appropriate progress monitoring instrument, we start troubleshooting Action 3.3: Implement Instruction.

> **TROUBLESHOOTING TIP #9:**
>
> **Use the progress monitoring instrument that is closest to the student's grade-level skill.**

CHECKPOINT B—ACTION 3.3: IMPLEMENT INSTRUCTION

Maybe we picked the correct intervention, but something about how we are implementing it is getting in the way of our student benefiting from it. This troubleshooting section will focus on trying to identify whether and how the intervention is not being implemented correctly. To assist with this we will be using the fidelity checklist (Form 7.3) for implementing instruction, which covers the seven steps below.

- *Step 1*: Present a clear goal/objective for each lesson.
- *Step 2*: Give a reason for why learning the skill is important.
- *Step 3*: Show/demonstrate the skill and the criterion of acceptable performance.
- *Step 4*: Practice the skill with the student.
- *Step 5*: Observe the student performing the skill.
- *Step 6*: Provide immediate and explicit feedback about the performance.
- *Step 7*: Additional practice of the skill.

Step 1: Present a Clear Goal/Objective for Each Lesson

The practice of having a goal for each lesson forces us to think about and justify why we are spending time doing what we are doing. The goal for English language arts or math should be tied directly to the standards. However, if we cannot find a link in the standards, then it is time to think hard about what we are doing. We hope Ms. Smedley asks herself, "Why am I teaching this lesson?" If her answer is "I don't know," then we would want Ms. Smedley to rethink her entire lesson. What if her answer is "Because it is the next lesson in our book"? This may or may not be a good reason to teach a lesson depending on the lesson or the alignment of her book with the standards. However, if her reason for teaching a skill is truly because it comes next, then it makes the next part of her lesson (giving a reason for learning the skill) that much more challenging.

> **TROUBLESHOOTING TIP #10:**
>
> **Make sure the goal is a skill the student needs to learn.**

Step 2: Give a Reason for the Importance of Learning the Skill

If we can tell our students how a skill will help them become better at reading, math, or behavior, it gives them a reason to want to learn it. If we don't have a clear goal or objective for teaching our lesson, it is nearly impossible for us to give a good reason for why our students should learn the skill. In our example above about following the next lesson in the book, Ms. Smedley could find herself saying, "This will help you learn the next lesson in the book." This is not a very compelling argument for her students to learn something. Nor is it compelling for her as their teacher, since she cannot see the purpose for why she is teaching the lesson.

> **TROUBLESHOOTING TIP #11:**
>
> **If there isn't a clear reason for why the student needs to learn a skill, don't teach it.**

Step 3: Show/Demonstrate the Skill and the Criterion of Acceptable Performance

This is our opportunity to provide a clear model of what it looks like to perform the skill. This allows us to be as explicit as possible so our students have a clear idea of what we want them to do. Phrases we want to use include "Watch me first," "My

> **TROUBLESHOOTING TIP #12:**
>
> **Make sure all eyes are on you as you demonstrate the skill.**

FORM 7.3

Fidelity Checklist for Implementing the Seven Steps of Instruction

Step 1: Present goal/objective for lesson.	**YES NO**
Step 2: Give reason for learning the skill.	**YES NO**
Step 3: Demonstrate skill and criterion of acceptable performance.	**YES NO**
Step 4: Practice skill with student.	**YES NO**
Step 5: Observe student performance.	**YES NO**
Step 6: Provide immediate feedback.	**YES NO**
Step 7: Additional practice of skill.	**YES NO**

turn," and "Eyes on me first." These are key phrases we should use as we model first, before we ask our students to respond. This makes the next part of our lesson go much smoother.

Step 4: Practice the Skill with the Student

Once we demonstrate the skill, we will use a gradual release with the student so he first practices the skill with us. This can be accomplished by having him practice the skill along with us. We should use phrases like "Let's do it together," "Now we will do it at the same time," and "All together now."

> **TROUBLESHOOTING TIP #13:**
>
> **Use the same phrase each time you practice the skill together so students know when to tune in.**

Step 5: Observe the Student Performing the Skill

After the student practices the skill with us, we want to have him practice the skill without us. We should use phrases like "Now you try," "It's your turn," and "Show me how you would. . . ." These phrases let him know it's his turn to demonstrate the skill without us.

> **TROUBLESHOOTING TIP #14:**
>
> **Ask each student individually to provide the answer so you can check for understanding.**

Step 6: Provide Immediate and Explicit Feedback about the Performance

We want to let our students know how they are doing. We can accomplish this by using consistent words as we correct their behavior. For example, we can say, "Stop. Watch me. Now you try" or "Look at me. That is. . . . Now you do it." We don't need to use many words and we do not have to come out and say, "That's wrong" or "You made a mistake." However, we do need a phrase that will get our student's attention, like "Stop" or "Look at me," so that we can correct the mistake immediately and have him practice it so he can learn it correctly.

Step 7: Additional Practice of the Skill

This step involves additional learning opportunities that should include how we want students to use the skill within a larger context. If the only opportunity to practice the skill occurs within a limited context, then it is likely the student will not transfer the skill or be able to use it in other areas. This provides multiple opportunities for a student to practice the skill across different formats, will increase his opportunity to practice, and increase the likelihood that he will learn it.

> **TROUBLESHOOTING TIP #15:**
>
> **Provide a lot of practice across different types of tasks.**

If everything checks out with the implementation of the instruction, then it is time to move on to how we designed the instruction. This happens by moving back to troubleshoot Action 3.2: Design Instruction.

CHECKPOINT C—ACTION 3.2: DESIGN INSTRUCTION

To determine whether we designed the instruction appropriately we will use the fidelity checklist that goes along with the flower graphic in Figure 6.2 (Form 7.4). Remember, the three *F*'s and one *S* are listed below. We have already covered one *F* for Format under implement instruction. Now, we will focus on the rest of the petals.

- Frequency
- Focus
- Size
- Format (covered in implement instruction)

Frequency

There are three questions that go along with frequency. While it may seem silly to collect such obvious data, it is amazing how wrong we can be when we assume things like the number of instructional minutes per day, or the number of times per week we deliver intervention. As we all know, schools can be crazy busy places to work, and with the best intentions we often only make things happen some of the time instead of all of the time. It's easy to get away from us as our attention is drawn to more pressing concerns. The good news is, once we have determined the actual number of minutes per day and the number of days we are providing a specific intervention, it is an easy fix.

If we find we need to change the frequency of how we deliver our intervention we can think about doing this by changing our routine or schedule. For example, if Ms. Smedley has blocked off 40 minutes for an intervention and she starts her lesson by asking the students "What do you remember from the last time we worked together?" and it takes 10 minutes to get through each student trying to explain what they remember, she has just lost 10 minutes of instructional time. More important, Ms. Smedley probably did not learn very much about what her students remember about a particular skill. Her question is too broad and is likely to elicit responses like "I remember that Alex kept sneezing on me and it was grossing me out." Instead, she should ask questions that are specific to the skill. For example, if Ms. Smedley wants to know what her students remember about the short-*u* sound she can say, "Who remembers from last time the sound short-*u* makes?"

Related to the loss of instructional minutes is the number of days we provide an intervention. If the intervention is meant to occur three days a week and it is scheduled on Monday, Wednesday, and Friday, we need to determine whether it will consistently fit into the schedule on these days. What if we find out that assemblies, field trips, and other school activities often happen on Fridays and our students only get the intervention 50% of the time? An easy fix would be to pick another day or cut back on assemblies, field trips, and other school activities (yep, that'll go over well with the students). Frequency can often be tightened up by ensuring the maximum number of minutes each

> **TROUBLESHOOTING TIP #16:**
> **Pick days you know the students are usually at school.**

Fidelity Checklist for Designing Instruction

Dimension	Component	Desired Practice	Actual Practice
Frequency	Number of weeks		
	Days per week		
	Minutes per day		
Focus	Broad skill		
	Narrow skill 1		
	Narrow skill 2		
	Narrow skill 3		
Format	*See Fidelity Checklist for Implementing the Seven Steps of Instruction (Form 7.3)*		
Size	Students in group		

day are spent on instruction and the number of days that it happens is adhered to within our schedule and the students' availability.

Focus

> **TROUBLESHOOTING TIP #17:**
>
> **Only pick skills that can be identified in the Common Core State Standards or other standards.**

> **TROUBLESHOOTING TIP #18:**
>
> **Make sure the student practices the skill under many formats that also represent it being used in a broad skill set.**

Is the intervention focusing on a broad skill, narrow skill, or a combination of both? It is important to think about how our students will be using the skill within the broader context of the content area. By teaching skills in isolation, we run the risk of our students not being able to perform the skill outside a narrow set of parameters. For example, if Hubert is learning to add two-digit numbers and he only practices using one format (horizontal or vertical) he may not be able to transfer this skill. That is, he may not know how to apply it if he sees it in another format or in a word problem. This is not the goal of learning, and we need to be careful when we implement interventions. We should remember to include practice within a broader skill set. Another consideration is to make sure the skill we pick is included within the standards.

Size

How many students are in the intervention group? The size of the group matters, and we know that research supports small groups (three to five students) over one-on-one instruction. How many students are too many for an intervention group? Ten or more students is probably getting to be too big, as it is hard for us to provide guidance and explicit feedback. As we think about available resources, we should consider grouping our students who have similar needs and scheduling them together. We can even coordinate this with another

> **TROUBLESHOOTING TIP #19:**
>
> **Share students with other teachers so that interventions can be provided in small groups at the same time.**

teacher so that she can work with a different group of students at the same time. If we plan our intervention time so that we can share students across grade levels, we can meet the needs of more students without having to duplicate intervention groups.

Format

We already covered this in the seven steps we use when implementing instruction in Action 3.3. Once we have plucked off all of the petals from the flower and have determined that things are as they should be, we can troubleshoot Action 2.1: Generate Assumed Causes of Phase 2 of the CBE process.

CHECKPOINT D—ACTION 2.1: GENERATE ASSUMED CAUSES

To refresh your memory, this action is about generating and testing assumed causes that are impeding the student from learning the desired skill. It is worthwhile to review some of the important features of this action, which can easily be accomplished by looking at Table 5.1 ("Rules for Developing Assumed Causes") summarized in the list below:

1. Focus on alterable skills.
2. Stick to essential tasks.
3. Prioritize problems.
4. Pick the most likely targets first.
5. Use skill sequences.

To troubleshoot assumed causes we are going to use the F.AC.T.R. worksheet from Phase 2 and go back through it while providing some helpful hints to consider as you review each step.

> **TROUBLESHOOTING TIP #20:**
>
> **The assumed cause should always be a prerequisite to the skill the student needs to learn.**

(F) Fact

A statement that defines the problem as the difference between the desired state and the student's performance (the CAP). This gives a clear under-

> **TROUBLESHOOTING TIP #21:**
>
> **Just because something can be changed and taught does not mean it needs to be.**

standing of the problem and its magnitude. If we are teaching a skill in reading or math and we can't find it within the CCSS for English language arts or mathematics, we should stop teaching it. This means we have not found the standard or desired state that we hope the student will achieve. For other content areas, we might need to refer to the state or district standards, or standards from the curriculum itself. If we cannot find the standards, then we haven't found the correct skill to teach.

> **TROUBLESHOOTING TIP #22:**
>
> **If you can't determine a source for why you are teaching the skill, then you don't have a desired state you should be teaching.**

(AC) Assumed Cause

This relates to the prerequisite skill causing the problem. The assumed cause is generally a skill the student was expected to have already learned but did not. By teaching this prerequisite skill, we can move to teaching more complex skills. One way to identify the prerequisite skills for reading and math is to use the CCSS to identify the skills that occur prior to this skill. Another troubleshooting activity is to stop and make sure we have eliminated some obvious causes.

Some of these might be that our student can hear and see well. It could also be more complex, but still obvious like confusing common letter sounds such as /s/ and /z/ or /f/ and

/v/. He might not know the difference between voiced and unvoiced sounds that are easily confused. Another example is if the student is having difficulty reading multisyllabic words. Maybe he doesn't know how to chunk words into syllables. For example, if we ask him how many syllables are in a word and he doesn't know the answer, we can show him how to rest his hand below his chin and say a word. Every time his jaw drops, that indicates a syllable.

> **TROUBLESHOOTING TIP #23:**
>
> **Look for the obvious cause of the problem first.**

Prerequisite skills don't have to be lengthy lessons. However, we do need to identify them so that they can be taught and more complex skills can then be the focus of our instruction.

(T) Test

To determine whether we correctly identified the assumed cause, we need to test it. Using the example of voiced and unvoiced letters, we would give the student a sheet of letters and ask him to produce the sound for each letter. If he misses the fricatives (e.g., /f/, /v/) then we know we are on to something. In our example of identifying syllables, we can give him a

> **TROUBLESHOOTING TIP #24:**
>
> **If the data have been collected somewhere else—go get them before giving another test.**

sheet of multisyllabic words and ask him to mark where the syllables occur. We only need to confirm whether we identified it correctly or not. Once the assumed cause has been tested we can move onto the *R*—Results.

(R) Results

This includes determining whether our student mastered the prerequisite skill or we verified the assumed cause. The results hinge on being able to confirm that we have identified the problem. In the examples above, if we gave the student a sheet of letters and asked him

> **TROUBLESHOOTING TIP #25:**
>
> **Look at what the student produces to see if you can identify any consistent error patterns.**

to provide the sounds, and he missed only those that are fricatives, then we are on the right track. If he cannot identify syllables in words when we ask him to mark where the syllables occur on a page full of words, then we again have hit the mark.

If you have been successful in moving back through Action 2.1 using the F.AC.T.R. worksheet then there is only one last place to go to for troubleshooting. That's all the way back to Action 1.2: Define the Problem at the beginning of Phase 1 of the CBE process.

CHECKPOINT E—ACTION 1.2: DEFINE THE PROBLEM

If we have made it all the way back to this action through troubleshooting it is likely that we have missed the boat completely. However, it is still worth our time to troubleshoot. The things in Action 1.2 that need our attention can be broken down into three areas:

1. *Area*: Description of Student Performance
   - *Clarification*: Performance is observable and measurable.
     - *Check*: Dead-man, so-what, and stranger tests
2. *Area*: Standard of Student Performance
   - *Clarification*: Standard is meaningful.
     - *Check*: CCSS, state or district standards, published curriculum
3. *Area*: Difference between Standard and Student Performance
   - *Clarification*: Difference is verifiable.
     - *Check*: CAP, Benchmark

Let's tackle this from the top starting with the description of student performance. Using the worksheet for Action 1.2 (Form 7.5) we look at the first three questions that address whether the performance is observable and measurable. These take us back through the three tests of a good problem definition. Next, we answer the questions about the standard of student performance being meaningful, being explicit to identify the source of the standard and confirm its use. Last, we answer two questions regarding the difference between the standard and student performance. If we answer "yes," we keep moving on to the next question. If however, we answer "no" to any of the questions, we need to stop and fix it. If you can identify the problem here yourself, that is great; but often it is helpful to have someone "check your work." They can provide a fresh perspective, which can be key to troubleshooting.

If we troubleshoot all the way back to Action 1.2 and still cannot figure out what the issue is, it is time to bring in a team to assist. It might be that the student has some very unique characteristics that make it difficult for him to learn certain skills. However, it has been our experience that even in those extreme cases where the student does not respond to otherwise good instruction it is because we have not been able to nail down the correct prerequisite skill needed to build upon. Often these students have instructional skills that look more like Swiss cheese, as they tend to learn some things really well, and it leads us to assume a large set of prerequisite skills are intact when in fact they are missing many skills. The best way to tackle this is to give an assessment that includes many discrete skills, like a mixed-math sheet or a spelling test to measure many decoding skills. This allows us to look at many skills at one time and to examine it for error patterns.

CHAPTER SUMMARY

Troubleshooting is something we encourage people to do when they have worked hard with a student and are not seeing the results they expect. The more people that can be involved in the process, the better; particularly for students whose problems tend to stump us despite our best efforts. As an example, one of us worked with a student who was making excellent progress at the end of the school year on decoding words and reading text at an appropriate rate and level of accuracy. When school began again in the fall, we used the same instructional strategies that worked the previous year. However, based on his lack of progress on

Worksheet for Troubleshooting Action 1.2: Defining the Problem

1. Is the performance observable and measurable?	**1. Dead-Man Test:** Is there an action word used to describe the student's performance like: *read, sound out, calculate, write, spell, produce, verbalize, demonstrate* . . . ?	**YES NO**
	2. So-What Test: Can you find this performance listed in the standards or anywhere else that can demonstrate that they are important enough to teach . . . ?	**YES NO**
	3. Stranger Test: If someone who does not know the student reads the statement regarding the student's performance, he/she would also agree that it is critical enough to teach ("so what"), and it requires the student to do something ("dead man") . . .	**YES NO**
2. Is the standard of student performance meaningful?	**1.** The standard is found in the Common Core State Standards . . .	**YES NO**
	2. The standard is found in the state or district standards . . .	**YES NO**
	3. The standard is clearly found in the published curriculum used to teach the subject . . .	**YES NO**
3. Is the difference verifiable between the standard and student performance?	**1.** There is a real and measurable difference between the standard and the student performance . . .	**YES NO**
	2. The difference is based on a reasonable (research-based) benchmark . . .	**YES NO**

the progress monitoring instruments, we found out that not only did these strategies seem to be ineffective, but he seemed to have lost a lot of the skills he had previously mastered. It was much greater than the typical summer regression. Instead of going back through the CBE process, we called his parents and found that he was in a bicycle accident at the beginning of summer and sustained a severe head injury. Clearly, this was an important piece of information that had implications for which prerequisite skills to assess and instructional strategies to use. Without it, we might have spent numerous hours focusing on other things assuming that he had not sustained a closed-head injury. The situation served as a reminder to us to always ask questions because you just might be surprised by the answers.

CHAPTER 8

Keeping the CBE Process Going

By now, you understand the importance of using the CBE process to assist students. What you still might be scratching your head about is how to get it going in your school and then keeping it going. We won't lie and say "Just give it a try—it's easy." However, we will say, "We have some secrets to share that will help you use CBE in your school." What follows are suggestions for you to consider to use before, during, and after initial implementation of CBE. We also provide hints for how to get CBE up and running and hints for keeping it going once you have started. At the end of this chapter there is also a question-and-answer section related to conducting CBE that you might find helpful.

DEVELOPING A PLAN FOR USING CBE

So you have decided to implement CBE so that you can better determine what skills students need in order to succeed in school and life. The exciting part is, if done well, CBE might just be the most powerful practice you will ever engage in during your teaching experience. This is because CBE provides explicit actions to take so that you ask the right questions, gather the right data, identify the right problems, and apply the right interventions—all while using the right progress monitoring instruments to measure student growth. How do you do it? With careful planning every step of the way. Thinking about CBE as what you need to do before, during, and after implementation allows you to focus on manageable chunks of the process. These chunks are divided into nine nice steps.

Before

Step 1: At What Level Will the Process Be Used?

This depends on who has the knowledge and experience to work through the CBE phases. You want to stack the deck in your favor; thinking about how it might best be implemented will help you determine at what level to start.

- *Classroom level.* Is this something that only one teacher is interested in? If yes, then this teacher will need to be able to work through the phases on her own without the assistance of others in the school or district. This is often difficult to do if no one else is there to help out.
- *Grade level.* Is this something a grade level is interested in doing? If yes, the teachers in that grade should understand that they will need to support each other as they learn the process and become familiar with the actions. They will have a larger network to rely on when they get stuck, which will be very helpful in keeping CBE going.
- *School level.* Is this something the school is interested in doing? If yes, all teachers in the school should be able to provide support and help each other as they look at individual student needs. Conducting CBE at the school level will help you find students with similar needs. This allows you to combine resources and address multiple students at one time.
- *District level.* Is this something the district is interested in doing? If yes, then the ability to support teachers across buildings and to home in on professional development needs for staff around particular interventions for students has just increased significantly. If multiple schools share a similar need around particular interventions for students, district leaders can now think about how to support teachers across buildings using common instructional strategies rather than leaving each school to figure it out on their own.

Step 2: Which Content Will You Focus on First?

While we know the skills students need varies greatly, it would be wise to concentrate on a particular content area like reading, math, or behavior at first until the CBE process is more familiar. Trying to do everything all at once will likely lead to frustration and people becoming overwhelmed. This increases the chances of abandoning the CBE process. It takes time and many attempts before people feel proficient at conducting CBE, and it is much easier if the content stays the same at least for the first half of the year while people are still learning how to do CBE.

What will the content area be? Our suggestion for choosing the content area should consider the following three things:

1. *Which content areas are most students struggling with?* Looking at testing data like universal screening and outcome assessment can give you a good idea of what

content areas have the most and the least number of proficient students. If more than 90% of students are proficient in math and only 70% are proficient in reading, it would seem to make more sense to start with reading.

2. *Which content area has interventions that have been proven effective?* If you already have progress monitoring data collected for students who are receiving certain interventions, then you can use this to determine which intervention has been producing the best results. It would be the one where students have improved the most. If you do not have these data, then identifying those interventions that have an evidence base would be the best place to start. Evidence based implies that someone else has collected data that shows students improve when they receive the intervention.

3. *In which content area do you have the most highly qualified teachers teaching?* Can you identify someone in the building who already has expertise in a content area and is available to help others? For example, is there a reading specialist or coach who is already working in the building and who could help with the identification and implementation of particular interventions? Having an expert already identified will aid in the implementation of CBE.

Step 3: Do You Have the Materials You Need?

This refers to the stuff you will need in order to work through each phase of CBE. Making sure the materials that are necessary to conduct CBE at each phase will help you determine in which content areas and grade levels you might be ready to embark on implementing CBE. Materials that you will need to consider having for each phase are:

- *Phase 1 materials*: Screening data, standards to judge skills against, matrix to collect RIOT and SCIL information.
- *Phase 2 materials*: Identification of priority skills within standards, sheet for F.AC.T.R., additional assessment instruments identified in the content area (if needed).
- *Phase 3 materials*: Interventions for specific skills, progress monitoring instruments, and graphs for progress monitoring data.

Step 4: When Will Implementation Start?

Timing is everything, so planning ahead of when you would like to start using CBE will be helpful. Because it takes a lot of legwork to gather the right data to help answer the right questions it is worth it to consider some of the following suggestions.

- *Fall.* Is this something that can happen right away, possibly after the first round of universal screening data has been collected? This will mean planning starting with day 1 of the school year. This might be difficult to do until you can clearly determine what some of the students' needs will be.
- *Winter.* This occurs after the first and possibly the second rounds of universal screen-

ing data have been collected. This allows you to have more data on any particular student and a group of students. However, it may also mean delaying working with a student who is in desperate need of some help.

- *After universal screening, and some collection of progress monitoring data.* This would provide multiple data points to use for the student and could be implemented at any time during the year when needed. This one gets our vote.

Steps 1 through 4 all happen *before* conducting CBE. Now we will address steps 5 through 8 that should occur *during* CBE.

During

Step 5: Who Will Manage the Materials That Need to Be Collected?

There are multiple pieces of data and other things that need to be collected throughout the CBE process. Having certain people designated for certain data sources can speed things along. Here's how you might want to organize this.

The list of data and things you will need to collect can be broken down into each phase. Having certain people responsible for gathering certain parts helps spread the workload, and it allows multiple people to become familiar with a student, increasing the chances of helping the student. Form 8.1 provides a handy checklist for making these decisions and having a document for reference.

Step 6: Who Will Summarize and Share the Data?

Once you have figured out who will help collect all of the data and other things that are needed to conduct CBE, you need to determine who will summarize and share the data. In order to help you think through this, you need to consider the skills that are required for this task. This person would ideally already be experienced in looking at data and sharing it in ways that are organized and make sense to others. We offer the following points to consider when identifying who this person or people might be.

- *Teacher working with the student.* While it may seem intuitive to have the person who is currently working with the student be the one to summarize and share the data, this person may be too close to the situation and cannot pull the information together that will help others think about the student. Sometimes it is best to have a fresh perspective when sharing the data. This allows the person to ask questions in a way that highlights new things to think about and ways to assist in helping the student.
- *Someone who is unfamiliar to the student.* This person may be a school psychologist or instructional coach who is skilled in sharing data and the CBE process but does not know the student. The pros to this are that this person can present information in an objective way, since she has no prior knowledge about the student. She might

"Person Responsible" Lists for Implementing CBE

CBE Phase 1: Fact Finding	
Source	**Person Responsible**
Cumulative folder	
Universal screening data	
Progress monitoring data	
End of grade/course test scores (e.g., statewide tests)	
Health, vision, hearing screening results	
Report cards	
Work samples	
Interview with current/previous teacher(s)	
Interview parent(s)/student	
Classroom observation	
Intervention plans and reports	
External reports (physicians, psychologist, physical therapist, etc.)	
IEP, IFSP, 504 plan	
RIOT/SCIL matrix	
Standards for skills of interest	

CBE Phase 2: Table of Things to Collect	**Person Responsible**
Source	
F.AC.T.R. Worksheet	
Additional assessments (if needed)	

CBE Phase 3: Table of Things to Collect	**Person Responsible**
Source	
Interventions	
Progress monitoring materials	
Graph for progress monitoring data	

Troubleshooting	**Person Responsible**
Source	
Fidelity Checklist for Progress Monitoring (Form 7.1)	
Checklist for Monitoring Progress (Form 7.2)	
Fidelity Checklist for Implementing Instruction (Form 7.3)	
Fidelity Checklist for Designing Instruction (Form 7.4)	
Worksheet for Defining the Problem (Form 7.5)	

be able to see different patterns or issues that others might not see. The cons are that she doesn't know the student and might focus on the wrong aspects because she doesn't have any prior information to help guide her.

- *Someone who is familiar with the student, but not currently working with him.* This person could be an administrator, a teacher from the previous year, or someone who once worked with the student but has not seen him recently. The pros are that her prior experience with the student may help narrow down areas that deserve more attention. She might be able to share successes she has previously experienced when working with the student. The cons are that she might focus on the wrong information based on old knowledge of the student. This could delay how quickly the CBE process can be accomplished.

No matter who is responsible for summarizing and sharing the data, it is most critical that they have the organizational skills to pull all of this information together into one place. Having this information organized will allow the whole team to work through their questions and concerns about a student without having to hunt things down. This can be a huge time saver and aid in conducting CBE.

Step 7: Who Will Implement the Interventions?

Who works directly with the student to implement the intervention can be just as critical as determining what the intervention will be. A good rule of thumb to follow is that the students who need the most help get it from the most skilled teachers. It would not be appropriate to have a classroom volunteer helper run an intervention when she has not been trained as an educator. Things to consider include:

- Which teachers have the most expertise in this particular skill area?
- Which teachers have already been trained in this intervention?
- Which teachers have data showing students have made progress when they deliver this intervention?
- Which teachers already have a group up and running using this intervention that this student can join?

Step 8: Who Will Collect Progress Monitoring Data and Graph Them?

The act of data collection is so much more than getting a number from student responses and putting that number on a graph. The number is a real representation of student skill. Thought of in this way, it provides an opportunity for teachers to put their eyes and ears on what students do when they demonstrate skills. This opportunity is critical to understanding whether what we intended the student to do is what the student is actually able to do within a structured setting such as collecting progress monitoring data. Keeping this in mind, we offer some advice on who should collect progress monitoring data.

- *The teacher who is providing the instruction.* This is the person who most needs to figure out, and rather quickly, whether what she is doing is helping the student or not. Without having a way to formatively evaluate how the student is doing, it is all just guesswork. Therefore, having the person who is providing the instruction also collect the progress monitoring data is a good way to go.
- *The assistant or aid within the classroom.* This person would have direct contact with the student and teacher on a regular basis to share the progress monitoring data. The teacher might even be able to observe the student while the other person collects the data. The problem is that this person is just reporting back numbers on a graph, and the opportunity to see firsthand how the student is doing has been lost.
- *Someone outside the classroom.* This person would only interact with the student when progress monitoring data need to be collected. What gets lost is the opportunity to have the teacher directly involved with either collecting the data herself or at least observing the data collection when she can. The person outside the room may not be familiar with the student and may not know what skills the student is currently working on. All of that additional information that you can glean from working directly with the student is lost for the teacher who is providing the instruction when someone else comes in to collect the data.

We have made it through Steps 1–8 and now we can move onto the last step that should be considered *after* the CBE process.

After

Step 9: Who Will Help Troubleshoot?

If things are not going well, who is going to be the person responsible for helping troubleshoot the situation? Remember, troubleshooting doesn't take you back to the beginning of the CBE process, but rather to the last place you left within the CBE process, which is progress monitoring. From here, you work your way backward through important access points of the process. We have designed a lot of nice checklists to use when conducting troubleshooting. However, it is just as important to determine *who* will be responsible for using the checklists. The last section of Form 8.1 provides the list of checklists that you may need to use. A simple solution may be that the person who was originally responsible for gathering those data also uses the checklist. This will simplify trying to determine who does what, and it connects the troubleshooter with the tasks they are most likely familiar with.

HINTS ON HOW TO GET CBE GOING

There are many ways to approach getting CBE implemented in a classroom, grade, school, or district. The most effective way is to make sure you have a team of people who understand assessment, instruction, curriculum standards, and have some experience in looking at data to help inform instructional decisions. This does not have to be one or two people; it can be a team of people who all contribute the necessary skills needed to use the problem-solving framework outlined in CBE. So tips for getting people to work together to do CBE are:

- Make sure the building administrator(s) is involved from the start and understands the process.
- Understand that it is a process that provides clear actions in order to address a problem a student is having.
- Use data and good instructional practices (two things everyone should do more of).
- Encourage teamwork among people with specific skill sets who might otherwise not work together.
- Pool resources as you identify which groups of students might benefit from which interventions.
- Gather a database for students who have received particular interventions so the effects can be looked at over time.
- Collaborate so you can track and share successes of working with individuals or groups of students.

HINTS ON HOW TO KEEP CBE GOING

Planning ahead and having specific people in charge of specific tasks make the CBE process more efficient. It also shares the work and knowledge, which helps everyone involved. To help you think about what it would look like to plan ahead we have put together a list of activities and ideas to help.

- Keep the building administrators involved from day 1. Your best chances of keeping CBE going is if the administration sees value in the process.
- Print out the flowchart so everyone has a copy, or make a poster for the wall. Even better, save a tree and project it on a wall.
- Have the forms you will need already copied and have a plan for who you think is best to manage each task.
- Have a set time for planning and working together each week. Get these CBE dates on your calendar from the beginning of the year so people have it built into their schedules from the start.
- Share a personal success story about a student with colleagues. This will reward those working hard and entice those who might want to join in but have been hesitant.
- Share the responsibilities for keeping CBE going. It is a lot of work and well worth the effort—but it is also fair to share that work. This can be done on yearly, quarterly, or monthly bases. There is something to be said for consistency so changing roles too quickly should also be avoided.

FREQUENTLY ASKED QUESTIONS
ABOUT PLANNING AND CONDUCTING CBE

1. Do I have to do every action of the CBE process?

Yes and No. The only action that you might be able to skip is Action 2.3 (note the phrase "as needed" in its title). If you find that you have enough information related to assessment data gathered from the previous actions, then you do not need to gather additional data in Action 2.3. Otherwise you need to consider each action and perform it appropriately.

2. Can I get away with doing only one phase and not all three phases?

No. In order to make the best decisions for students, each phase must be used. We have heard teachers say they just want to implement an intervention and monitor progress because they have a "gut feeling" that this is what the student needs. Would you go to a doctor that provided you treatments based on nothing other than their "gut"? We wouldn't recommend it (even with a gastroenterologist). Each phase is meant to ensure that what we do with students is targeted to what they need.

3. As a special educator, will I be allowed to use CBE if the school doesn't use it?

Yes. CBE can be used individually by teachers with individual students or small groups of students with similar concerns. One of the biggest barriers to successful student outcomes is not knowing how to properly address areas of concern for students who struggle. CBE will allow you to address the needs of your students, and because this is your job, you should experience only encouragement to use CBE.

4. How can I persuade my school to adopt CBE or at least allow me to use it?

In the current age of accountability and the growing need to demonstrate outcomes we do not know of any administrator who is "not interested" or who would say no to the idea of making students more successful. One persuasive argument we have used is to inform the administrator/supervisor that we will collect and show them data on how the students are doing. If they are not satisfied with the growth and the efforts put into CBE, then we can find another process to use to help us problem-solve.

5. Can anyone do CBE?

Probably not. CBE is a process that requires technical skills, knowledge of content and interventions, and most of all, thinking. CBE is most successful when it is used by skilled individuals who are very familiar with the process. We do not recommend that CBE be used by anyone who is not fully trained and skilled with assessments, curriculum, and instructional techniques.

6. **Would it be a good idea to involve the parents of a struggling student to also conduct CBE at home, or should it only be done in the classroom?**

Given the technical skills to administer and analyze the assessment instruments, use curriculum, and implement good instructional techniques, this is a job best left to the professionals at school. "Don't try this at home!" should be the warning label on CBE. However, parents should know what interventions their child will be involved in and how their progress will be monitored. Additional activities related to the intervention that parents could do at home would be an appropriate way to include them. And parents should always be involved in and informed of the process of educating their children.

7. **Do I have to use CBM to monitor progress in Phase 3 of CBE?**

No. However, you do need to use a progress monitoring instrument that has the following characteristics:

- Enough equivalent forms that it can be given daily or weekly.
- Evidence that it is sensitive to student improvement (usually provided by calculating the reliability of slope).
- Time efficient to administer and score (usually under 5 minutes).

We recommend CBM because it meets these characteristics.

CHAPTER SUMMARY

Many steps can be preplanned to aid in the successful implementation of CBE. Breaking things into what needs to happen before, during, and after is one way to ensure that the people involved do not get overwhelmed. It also allows things to be done in stages and to prioritize how to proceed. Our best advice for conducting CBE is to do it as a team so that the work is shared and the problem-solving process is truly collaborative. We can learn a lot from each other if we allow ourselves the time to ask the right questions and gather the right information to help all educators help students succeed in school and life.

CHAPTER 9

Conclusion

In this book, we have covered many ideas and practices. We started with basic ideas and concepts of evaluation and their place within education. Then, because our focus is on planning effective instruction, we moved to the topic of CBE and how it is used in education. We also emphasized the notion of using data to drive both the questions we ask and the decisions we make. Thinking about questions and decision making led us to the CBE inquiry process.

Throughout the book we have tried to explain and show you how CBE is used to make decisions about both *what* and *how* to teach students who are struggling across areas of academic concern. It is now time to step back and refocus on the bigger frame of CBE. We can do that by asking two questions:

1. Why would you want to use CBE? (or work with colleagues who use CBE?)
2. How do you actually employ CBE?

That is, what can you really gain from correct implementation of CBE practices in your classroom and school? These are important questions that relate to the time, efficiency, and effectiveness of our efforts to carry out the social imperative of having all students succeed in their educational endeavors.

Accountability for positive educational results is more important than ever. Today students of all backgrounds and subgroups are required to overcome obstacles in learning and show performance gains. Without doubt, there is a new emphasis on achievement in academic and social behavior, and the stakes for underachievement are now extraordinarily high for teachers and schools. Also, we must recognize both the frequency and impact of underachievement on our communities and the nation (due to the impact on employability, work skills, and overall societal literacy about the world we live in). Therefore, the effectiveness of educational systems is now under increased scrutiny. CBE is one of the processes that will allow teachers, schools, and districts to get better student results. CBE cannot solve every problem, but it can provide the information required to determine what to teach and who should be taught (i.e., students with major performance difficulties).

In the educational world, efficiency is of utmost importance. The "shelf life" of a student is about 13 years total. Early childhood education and strong foundational instruction in the critical area of literacy must be compressed into the first few of those 13 years. This is necessary so that students can begin to learn from texts and outside of active classroom instruction.

This is why the need for prevention and for early intervention has long been understood. These concerns are especially pronounced for students who may come to their educational experience with compromised readiness for success (for any number of reasons).

At the same time (and perhaps due to those concerns listed above), the educational community has continued to experience increased pressure for teachers and students to produce and maintain high levels of competence/achievement. This means the educational community must:

- Understand why students struggle to learn.
- Use more efficient processes to increase student success.
- Add new and/or increasingly complex content into the school day.

We believe it is fair to assume the following to be true in most educational units today:

Everyone in education is busy!
Everyone is feeling the pinch of too many masters and too little time.

This means there is no time for random educational processes or for systems to be uninformed about how to address the needs of struggling students. Time is passing! We need an organized, focused, precise, and *relentless* approach in order to obtain educational success for all students in our classrooms. Because we know no single curriculum or instructional process will give us all of these for every student, we also understand that schools need mechanisms that produce focus, efficiency, and effectiveness.

For example, many schools now engage in Professional Learning Communities to address the diverse educational needs of their students. Other schools have looked to the use of data teams to increase student performance at instructional, grade, school, and district levels. Yet other schools/districts are adopting system-level solutions such as RTI or MTSS as a means to provide good core instruction for all students while also meeting the needs of students who previously were left to struggle alone with the core demands.

It is unfortunate that these potentially powerful approaches typically don't come with mechanisms to tell us where previous instruction broke down, where future instruction needs to be focused, and what instruction can meet most students' needs. Although school staff across the United States have come to realize that research-based practices must be a foundation of practice in our schools, there is less understanding of the need for supplemental or intensive instruction/interventions that must also be research based and use effective practices.

We have seen an increase in the number of "researched" practices and "effective" programs on the market. There is little question that many of these programs, strategies, and practices can have some positive effect in addressing the needs of struggling learners as a group. But the real issue is knowing which effective practices to use, given the specific and unique characteristics of individual students or groups of students. It will never be efficient, or sufficient, to apply research-based practices validated on groups without an understanding of which programs align with characteristics of specific tasks and students. Educators must know the evolving curriculum that students are expected to learn as well as the most effective instructional approaches required to teach that content. They also need to know how to determine exactly what individual students currently do and do not know. This is the only information that can tell us which students do, or do not, need to be taught a given objective on any given day (and when to move on once that objective has been learned).

Analyzing the process of learning is critical. Without that we don't know how to teach. However, although this may seem obvious, analyzing both the curriculum and instructional procedures is just as important! This is why a reliable and precise process for coming to understand learning problems within the context of the curriculum is of utmost value. Without it we are relegated to the uncertainty of trial and error. We do what has possibly worked in the past, or we simply pick something that "seems like the right thing to do."

Obviously, educators, students, and parents deserve an educational problem-solving process that will provide precise and reliable data. But they also need the ability to link both assessments and instructions to what students need to learn. CBE, and the inquiry process it details, provides that mechanism for solving learning problems quickly, easily, and (most important) accurately.

CBE provides a system of inquiry that allows you to link and then address student concerns (individually or in groups). When you find those problems and concerns, you have a defined way to address them by way of systematic instruction.

The things you have learned in this book will allow you to focus your efforts on the most important questions in order to find critical answers for how to make struggling learners more successful. With functional student information you will be in a more defensible position to make decisions and form future plans. CBE can maximize your instructional opportunities, allowing you to accomplish the results your students need and schools are increasingly required to show. The strong foundation in the principles of CBE you have gained from this book will allow you to better understand what students' need. It will also allow you to plan and implement effective instruction.

We have no doubt that you will need to make the two decisions explained at the beginning of this chapter. We hope that the information presented throughout the book has provided you with the foundation to answer those questions. It is always there when you need a refresher or reinforcement. When working with your students, you still need to decide:

1. What to teach.
2. How to teach it.

We hope that we have now taken some of the mystery of that decision making out of your life. This book supplies you with a roadmap for success that should feed into your existing supports (such as PLCs, Data Teams, or your RTI/MTSS processes) by way of highly valued data for planning, teaching, monitoring, and measuring success.

So why do we think CBE is so important and necessary for educators like you? We think CBE will make you an even more successful teacher! You see that education is about your students and their right to a successful educational experience *tomorrow*, and you want to be the one to guide them down that road to long-term success.

Glossary

Accomplishment: Achieving or reaching a goal.

Alignment: Multiple procedures or aspects focusing on the same topic, content, or level of performance. Alignment among curriculum, instruction, and assessment generally means that they focus on the same content and the same (or similar) characteristics.

Alterable: Able to be changed. Instruction should focus on things that are alterable because trying to change things that can't be changed is frustrating.

Alterable variables: Characteristics of the setting, curriculum, instruction, or learner that educators can reasonably change.

Assessment: The process of collecting information for use in evaluation. Assessment can be carried out by reviewing products, interviewing, observing, and/or testing.

Assessment questions: Any question for which we collect information to answer. These are also sometimes called the purposes of assessment.

Assumed causes: Hypothesized explanations for student learning or behavior problems.

Automaticity: An accurate response performed at a high rate with distractions present. Automaticity is generally considered to be the highest level of proficiency.

Concepts: A collection of defining characteristics that a set of objects, events, actions, or situations share.

Criterion of acceptable performance: The standards for how well (accurately, frequently, or to what quality) a behavior should be performed by a student who has finished instruction on a task.

Criterion-referenced: Performance on an instrument that is compared to a criterion.

Curriculum: The content taught in a class. It is not synonymous with the published materials used in a class or the teacher's approach to delivery of instruction.

Curriculum-based assessment (CBA): Approaches to collecting information to make educational decisions that rely on students performing tasks that are included in the curriculum. It also describes a specific approach to instructional decision making that focuses on accurate performance of discrete tasks in sequence.

Curriculum-based evaluation (CBE): A structured instructional decision-making process that relies on a heuristic overlay that can be applied to various content areas. It is also the reason you bought this book.

Curriculum-based measurement (CBM): An evidence-based approach to assessing student performance that is standardized, based on production of a skill, is sensitive to growth, and is an indicator of performance on a broader outcome.

Curriculum derived: Materials used for assessment that are taken directly from the curriculum materials that are used for instruction.

Curriculum independent: Materials used for assessment that are not taken from the curriculum materials used for instruction. Also called generic probes, passages, or materials.

Data: Information that is quantitative in nature. The term "data" is plural. "Datum" is the singular. Therefore, "Data are plural."

Data poor: Not having enough good information to answer the questions and make the decisions that will allow you to improve student outcomes.

Data rich: Having a lot of information available; not necessarily good information.

Dead-man test: A way to evaluate a problem definition, goal, or objective to ensure that it contains action words. It consists of considering whether a dead man can do it.

Decision: In this book, it refers to a choice made about student performance or educational need, in particular as it is relevant to plan or evaluate instruction.

Decision fatigue: When making a decision becomes increasingly difficult due to the number of decisions one has already made. Just like muscles become fatigued from continued use, the more decisions one makes the more difficult it becomes to make additional decisions.

Diagnostic decisions: Decisions about what skills or knowledge a student has not yet mastered to determine what to teach.

Differentiated instruction: Teaching that is aligned with each individual student's educational needs. Students with similar needs can receive group instruction, but each student receives what he or she needs.

Disconfirming evidence: Information that contradicts a hypothesis or conclusion.

Effect size: A metric that indicates the strength of evidence for an intervention or instructional method. There are different standards for judging different effect sizes.

Empirically derived: Determined through a process of high-quality research.

Evaluation: The process by which educators come to make decisions by using their judgment to make inferences about information and answer questions.

Evidence: The information gathered and used to make a decision.

Evidence based: Interventions or instructional approaches that are based on empirical research that demonstrates the efficacy of that specific program or product.

Experts: People who are very proficient at a task or very knowledgeable in a field.

Facts: Discrete pieces of knowledge that can stand in isolation. They can be known without understanding or meaning. Also sometimes called declarative knowledge.

Focus: The content of interest in intervention or instruction.

Format: The characteristics of how instruction is delivered.

Formative assessment: Assessment that is designed to collect information that can be used to plan instruction. Also called formative evaluation and considered assessment *for* learning.

Frequency: The number of times something occurs. One usage is the number of times a behavior occurs during a time interval (usually minutes). A second is how often a student receives instruction or intervention.

General outcome measures (GOM): A type of curriculum-based assessment that uses a task that is a robust indicator of overall performance in a content area. GOMs are of particular value for screening and monitoring progress because they are indicators of proficiency and sensitive to change toward long-term goals.

Generative approach: An approach to instruction in which the student induces, or generates, the outcome. The teacher serves as a facilitator or guide to varying degrees.

Glossary: A list of terms at the back of a book that provides definitions for unusual or difficult words or expressions.

Goal: A level of performance that a student is expected to reach within a certain time frame. Also called an objective, learning target, or outcome.

Goal line: A line connecting baseline or pretest performance to the goal. It provides a visual representation of the average change in performance (i.e., rate of progress) expected.

Heuristic overlay: An overlay technique is a set of assessment rules and strategies that can be used on any set of materials or content.

Individualized assessment: Choosing assessment procedures that will provide the specific information needed to make decisions about a particular student or group of students. It does not mean that different materials or procedures are used with each individual. Standardized procedures and materials should still be used when appropriate or necessary.

Individualized instruction: Teaching that is specifically tailored to meet a student's particular educational needs. It does not mean one-to-one instruction. A teacher may employ individualized instruction by teaching a group of students who have the same educational need.

Inference: Developing conclusions from a body of evidence. The evidence doesn't tell exactly what the conclusion should be, so inference is the distance between the content of the evidence and the conclusion drawn.

Information: Knowledge that can be collected, summarized, and used as the basis for decision making.

Instruction: Characteristics of teaching that can be altered to improve student learning.

Instruments: Any product or procedure that can be used to collect information. Also called tools and sometimes more broadly referred to as tests (which are one specific instance) or assessments (more descriptive of the process).

Interview: An assessment procedure by which an educator can collect relevant information by asking questions of appropriate people such as other educators, students, and parents.

Judgment: The quality of deciding. Good judgment is generally equated to positive outcomes of decisions.

Learned helplessness: The tendency to act as if one has no control over a situation or outcome that has developed over time.

Learner: The individual or group of students being instructed and who is/are the focus of our problem solving efforts. It's all about the students.

Learning orientation: The belief that success comes with perseverance toward achieving a goal.

Learning preferences: That individuals prefer certain characteristics of instruction or content over others.

Learning styles: The flawed notion that some fixed capacities or sensory modes work better for learning than others for individuals.

Learning target: (see *Goal*).

Mastery measure: A type of curriculum-based assessment that measures a discrete or specific skill. They can be used for short-term monitoring and determination of proficiency on discrete skills, but are not useful for long-term progress monitoring.

Measurement: The assignment of numerical values to objects or events according to rules.

Measurement drift: An individual's application or administration of an instrument changing over time. It is generally not noticed by the individual, but can be countered with periodic refresher training.

Metacognition: An individual's awareness of and control over his or her own thinking.

Motivation: A drive toward achieving certain goals that elicits certain behaviors or actions.

Muti-tier system of supports (MTSS): A systemwide approach that includes both response to intervention (RTI) for academics and positive behavioral interventions and supports (PBIS) for behavior.

Norm referenced: Performance on an instrument that is compared to that of a referent group of peers or similar individuals.

Objective: (see *Goal*).

Observe: An assessment procedure by which information is collected by watching and recording characteristics of individuals or environments.

Performance orientation: The belief that success comes from completing tasks rather than achieving goals.

Perseverance: Continuing on a course of action toward achieving a goal.

Positive behavioral interventions and supports (PBIS): A systemic educational approach that relies on aligning evidence-based strategies with student need to effect positive behavior outcomes.

Precision teaching: A method of instruction that is based on applied behavior analysis. It focuses on direct observations of behavior and measurement of frequency plotted on celeration charts.

Prerequisite: A skill that must be mastered in order to learn or master a more complex one.

Prior knowledge: The best single predictor of learning success. Prior knowledge is what a person knows about a task, or its prerequisites, before the lesson begins. When an evaluator summarizes a student's current level of performance, she is reporting the student's relevant prior knowledge.

Probability: The likelihood that something will happen or is true.

Problem analysis: A stage of problem solving in which the problem is broken down into its component parts (generally through a task analysis and direct assessment).

Problem identification: A stage of problem solving in which the problem is explicitly identified and defined. This sets the stage for problem analysis and solution.

Problem solution: A stage of problem solving to implement strategies to address the reason the problem is occurring that was identified during problem analysis.

Problem solving: A systematic approach to specifying a problem and developing a solution. Methods of problem solving generally include similar stages of identification, analysis, and solution, although some include additional components.

Procedures: A series of steps for performing a task and the rules for when to apply them.

Proficiency: The level of performance necessary for consideration that the student has mastered a skill to satisfactorily perform the next skill in the skill sequence.

Progress monitoring: Assessment conducted by taking repeated measures of performance over time.

Relevant: Having a direct impact on student learning.

Research based: Interventions or instructional approaches that are based on empirical research that demonstrates the importance or efficacy of a component, but not the entire package.

Response to intervention (RTI): A systemic educational approach that relies on aligning evidence-based instruction with student need and uses universal screening and progress monitoring to make data-based decisions. Intervention is provided in tiers of support to evaluate whether the instruction provided is increasing student learning.

Review: An assessment procedure by which prior products and documents are examined and relevant information recorded.

RIOT: An acronym for the categories of assessment procedures. These are Review, Interview, Observe, and Test. Each of these four can be used to collect information relevant for making decisions in order to plan instruction.

Saturation: A hypothetical point when one has enough information to maximize good judgment and collecting additional information will not improve decision making.

SCIL: An acronym for evaluation domains. These are Setting, Curriculum, Instruction, and Learner. Each of these are levels of potential intervention and aggregation at which intervention may be provided.

Setting: The location where learning is to take place. Also sometimes called the environment or the instructional environment.

Size: The number of students in an instructional group.

So-what test: A way of determining the validity of a problem definition, goal, or objective by determining whether it is something worth teaching or doing.

Standard treatment protocol: An approach to response to intervention (RTI) that uses a consistent set of methods or strategies for students who need supplemental or intensive intervention.

Standards: Descriptors or levels of performance that are expected to be achieved at a certain time point, such as a grade level.

Stranger test: A way of determining the clarity of a problem definition, goal, or objective by having someone else read it to determine whether he or she could assess or teach it.

Summative assessment/evaluation: Assessment or evaluation that takes place at the end of a period of time such as a unit or section of instruction. Summative assessment/evaluation "sums up" the learning and is sometimes called assessment *of* learning.

Supplantive approach: An approach to teaching through which the teacher actively adds to the student's knowledge through direct or explicit instruction. Supplantive instruction is hands-on.

Task analysis: The process of breaking a skill down into its component parts that must be mastered in order to perform it proficiently.

Technical adequacy: Characteristics of an assessment procedure that give it the properties of being able to do what we expect it to do. These are broadly defined as reliability (or consistency) and validity (or accuracy). For interviews, representativeness is also included.

Test: An assessment procedure to determine how a child functions by having him perform a selected sample of actions that represent the desired content.

Tiered instruction: Instruction that is provided in levels of increasing intensity, often called core, supplemental, and intensive.

Tool skill: A skill that is an essential subtask of many other skills.

Tools: (see *Instruments*).

Trend line: The slope in the student's learning as seen on a chart, with time on one axis and performance on the other. It is the average rate of progress the student is making.

Unalterable: Not able to be changed. Instruction should *not* focus on things that are unalterable because trying to change them will be frustrating.

Universal screening: Brief assessment that is done with all students in a grade or school to determine which students are on track for proficiency and which need additional instruction.

Zone of distal development: The skills that a student cannot yet perform. Also sometimes called the frustrational range.

Zone of proximal development: The skills that a student can perform with guidance. Also sometimes called the instructional range.

Resources

Best Evidence Encyclopedia

www.bestevidence.org

- Free website created by the Johns Hopkins University School of Education's Center for Data-Driven Reform in Education (CDDRE).
- It offers information about the strength of the evidence supporting a variety of programs available for students in grades K–12.

Center on Instruction

www.centeroninstruction.org

- Free website that provides a collection of scientifically based research and information on birth–12 instruction in reading, math, science, special education, and English language learning.
- It offers materials and resources on these subjects including professional development models.

Center on Teaching and Learning—University of Oregon

http://ctl.uoregon.edu

- Free website with resources for reading, spelling, mathematics, and selected content areas for students.
- It offers curriculum maps, guides to review core reading programs and supplemental and intervention programs, and guides for how to teach skills along with assessments and benchmarks.

Evidence Based Intervention Network–University of Missouri

http://ebi.missouri.edu

- Free website that reviews the literature for evidence-based interventions and categorizes each intervention based on the common problem for which it has been validated.
- It offers a collection of intervention briefs and related videos.

153

Educational Research Newsletter

www.ernweb.com

- Free website that provides educators with recent research on reading, math, behavior management, and raising student achievement.
- It offers brief reports on the most useful and relevant findings from leading journals and organizations.

Florida Center for Reading Research

www.fcrr.org

- Free website provides information about reading instruction and assessments for students PreK–12th grade.
- It offers downloadable reading activities including materials and directions for delivering instruction related to targeted reading skills.

Intervention Central

www.interventioncentral.org/home

- Free website with resources for academic and behavioral interventions as well as assessments.
- It offers downloadable publications on effective teaching practices and tools that streamline classroom assessment and intervention.

IRIS Center—Vanderbilt University

http://iris.peabody.vanderbilt.edu

- Free website with resources for reading and math grades PreK–high school, RTI, behavior, and transition.
- It offers resources for each area that includes modules, case studies, and information briefs. Many of the forms are available in Spanish.

Learning Point Associates (merged with American Institutes for Research)

www.learningpt.org

- Free and for-fee website has publications about education issues from leadership to the classroom.
- It offers publications related to after-school programs, literacy, district and school improvement, and educator effectiveness.

National Center on Intensive Intervention (NCII)

www.intensiveintervention.org

- Free website with resources for reading, math, and behavior K–12.
- It offers tool charts for interventions and assessments, reports available on interventions, free monthly newsletter.

National Center on Response to Intervention

www.rti4success.org

- Free website with resources for reading and math K–12.
- It offers tool charts for assessments, training modules, webinars, and briefs related to the implementation of RTI.

Reading Rockets

www.readingrockets.org

- Free website with a focus on reading for PreK through elementary.
- It offers guidelines, resources, and videos about instructional materials, research, and other reading resource links geared toward teachers, parents, principals, librarians, and professionals.

RTI Action Network

www.rtinetwork.org

- Free website with a focus on implementation of RTI PreK–12 in reading, math, and behavior.
- It offers resources, guidelines, webinars, and research reports for teachers, parents, school leaders, and higher education faculty.

Vaughn Gross Center for Reading and Language Arts (Meadows Center for Preventing Educational Risk)

www.meadowscenter.org/vgc

- Free website with a focus on reading. This center is connected to the Meadows Center for Preventing Educational Risk (MCPER), which also has research related to academic, behavioral, and social skills for students with a focus on students with disabilities.
- It offers reading activities and PD guidelines for reading instruction for PreK through high school including ELL students, and students in special education.

What Works Clearinghouse

http://ies.ed.gov/ncee/wwc

- Free website supported by the U.S. Department of Education's Institute of Education Sciences that provides information on instruction with research-based recommendations for schools and classrooms.
- It offers reviews of research evidence on the effectiveness of interventions (programs, products, practices, and policies).

References

Adams, G. L., & Engelmann, S. (1996). *Research on direct instruction: 20 years beyond DISTAR*. Seattle: Educational Achievement Systems.

Ambrose, S. A., Bridges, M. W., DiPietro, M., Lovett, M. C., & Norman, M. K. (2010). *How learning works: Seven research-based principles for smart teaching*. San Francisco: Jossey-Bass.

Anderson, L. W., & Krathwohl, D. R. (Eds.). (2001). *A taxonomy for learning, teaching, and assessing: A revision of Bloom's taxonomy of educational objectives*. New York: Pearson.

Arter, J. A., & Jenkins, J. R. (1979). Differential diagnosis prescriptive teaching: A critical appraisal. *Review of Educational Research, 49,* 517–555.

Ashlock, R. B. (2009). *Error patterns in computation: Using error patterns to help each student learn* (10th ed.). New York: Pearson.

Ball, D. L., & Cohen, D. K. (1996). Reform by the book: What is—or might be—the role of curriculum materials in teacher learning and instructional reform? *Educational Researcher, 25*(9), 6–8.

Barbash, S. (2012). *Clear teaching: With direct instruction Siegfried Engelmann discovered a better way of teaching*. Arlington, VA: Education Consumers Foundation.

Black, P., & Wiliam, D. (1998). Inside the black box: Raising standards through classroom assessment. *Phi Delta Kappan, 80*(2), 139–144.

Bloom, B. S. (1980). The new direction in education research: Alterable variables. *Phi Delta Kappan, 61,* 382–385.

Borich, G. (2011). *Effective teaching methods: Research-based practice* (7th ed.). Boston: Pearson.

Burns, M. K., & Parker, D. C. (2014). *Curriculum-based assessment for instructional design*. New York: Guilford Press.

Cadwell, J., & Jenkins, J. (1986). Teacher's judgments about their students: The effect of cognitive simplification strategies on the rating process. *American Educational Research Journal, 23,* 460–475.

Campbell, N. R. (1940). *Final report, Committee of the British Association for Advancement of Science on the Problem of Measurement*. London: British Association.

Carbo, M. (1992). Giving unequal learners an equal chance: A reply to a biased critique of learning styles. *Remedial and Special Education, 13*(1), 19–39.

Carbonneau, N., Vallerand, R., & Lafreniere, M. (2012). Toward a tripartite model of intrinsic motivation. *Journal of Personality, 80,* 1147–1178.

Carter, K., Cushing, K., Sabers, D., Stein, P., & Berliner, D.C. (1988). Expert–novice differences in perceiving and processing visual classroom information. *Journal of Teacher Education, 39,* 25–31.

Chafouleas, S., Riley-Tillman, T. C., & Sugai, G. (2007). *School-based behavioral assessment: Informing intervention and instruction*. New York: Guilford Press.

Chan, L. K. (1996). Combined attributional training for seventh-grade average and poor readers. *Journal of Research in Reading, 19*(2), 111–127.

Connor, C., Morrison, F., Fishman, B., Schatschneider, C., & Underwood, P. (2007). The early years: Algorithm-guided individualized reading instruction. *Science, 315*(5811), 464–465.

Deno, S. L. (1985). Curriculum-based measurement: The emerging alternative. *Exceptional Children, 52,* 219–232.

Dev, P. (1997). Intrinsic motivation and academic achievement: What does their relationship imply for the teacher? *Remedial and Special Education, 18*(1), 12–19.

Dweck, C. (1986). Motivational processes affecting learning. *American Psychologist, 41*(10), 1040–1048.

Edwards, W. J., & Newman, R. J. (2000). Multiattribute evaluation. In T. Connolly, H. R. Arkes, & K. R. Hammond (Eds.), *Judgment and decision making: An interdisciplinary reader* (2nd ed., pp. 17–34). New York: Cambridge University Press.

Elbaum, B., Vaughn, S., Hughes, M., & Moody, S. W. (1999). Grouping practices and reading outcomes for students with disabilities. *Exceptional Children, 65,* 339–415.

Engle, R. A. (2006). Framing interactions to foster generative learning: A situative explanation of transfer in a community of learners classroom. *Journal of the Learning Sciences, 15*(4), 451–498.

Figlio, D. N., & Lucas, M. E. (2004). Do high grading standards affect student performance? *Journal of Public Economics, 88,* 1815–1834.

Flynn, L., Hosp, J., Hosp, M., & Robbins, K. (2011). Word recognition error analysis: Comparing isolated word list and oral passage reading. *Assessment for Effective Intervention, 36,* 167–178.

Fuchs, L. S., & Deno, S. L. (1991). Paradigmatic distinctions between instructionally relevant measurement models. *Exceptional Children, 57,* 488–501.

Geary, D. (1995). Reflections of evolution and culture in children's cognition. *American Psychologist, 50,* 1–38.

Gersten, R., & Dimino, J. (1993). Visions and revisions: A special education perspective on the whole-language controversy. *Remedial and Special Education, 14*(4), 5–13.

Giangreco, M. F., Edelman, S. W., Luiselle, T. E., & MacFarland, S. Z. C. (1997). Helping or hovering? Effects of instructional assistant proximity on students with disabilities. *Exceptional Children, 64,* 7–18.

Glass, G. V. (1983). Effectiveness of special education. *Policy Studies Review, 2,* 65–78.

Good, T., & Brophy, J. (2008). *Looking in classrooms* (10th ed.). Boston: Pearson.

Goodwin, J. S., & Goodwin, J. M. (1984). The tomato effect. *Journal of the American Medical Association, 251*(18), 2387–2390.

Greenwood, C. R. (1991). Longitudinal analysis of time, engagement and achievement in at-risk versus non-risk students. *Exceptional Children, 57,* 521–535.

Groopman, J. E. (2007). *How doctors think.* Boston: Houghton Mifflin.

Hemingway, Z., Hemingway, P., Hutchinson, N. L., & Kuhns N. A. (1987). Effects of student characteristics on teachers' decisions and teachers' awareness of these effects. *Journal of Special Education, 11,* 313–326.

Hosp, J. (2011). Using assessment data to make decisions about teaching and learning. In K. Harris, S. Graham, & T. Urdan (Eds.), *APA educational psychology handbook* (Vol. 3, pp. 87–110). Washington, DC: American Psychological Association.

Hosp, J. (2012). Formative evaluation: Developing a framework for using assessment data to plan instruction. *Focus on Exceptional Children, 44*(9), 1–11.

Hosp, M. K., Hosp, J. L., & Howell, K. W. (2007). *The ABCs of CBM: A practical guide to curriculum-based measurement.* New York: Guilford Press.

Howell, K. W., & Morehead, M. K. (1987). *Curriculum-based evaluation for special and remedial education: A handbook for deciding what to teach.* Columbus, OH: Merrill.

Howell, K. W., Fox, S. L., & Morehead, M. K. (1993). *Curriculum-based evaluation: Teaching and decision making.* Pacific Grove, CA: Brooks/Cole.

Howell, K. W., & Nolet, V. (2000). *Curriculum-based evaluation: Teaching and decision making* (3rd ed.). Belmont, CA: Wadsworth.

Johnson, K., & Street, E. (2012). *Response to intervention and precision teaching: Creating synergy in the classroom.* New York: Guilford Press.

Kavale, K. (1981). Functions of the Illinois Test of Psycholinguistic Abilities (ITPA): Are they trainable? *Exceptional Children, 47,* 496–510.

Lakin, K. C. (1983). A response to Gene V. Glass. *Policy Studies Review, 2,* 233–239.

Landfried, S. E. (1989). "Enabling" undermines responsibility in students. *Educational Leadership, 47*(3), 79–83.

Laufer, A. (1997). *Simultaneous management: Managing projects in a dynamic environment.* New York: American Management Association.

Leader, C. A. (1983). The talent for judgment. *Proceedings,* 49–53.

Lipman, P. (1997). Restructuring in context: A case study of teacher participation and the dynamics of ideology, race, and power. *American Educational Research Journal, 34,* 3–38.

Marzano, R. J., Brandt, R. S., Hughes, C. S., Jones, B. F., Presseisen, B. Z., Rankin, S. C., et al. (1988) *Dimensions of thinking*. Alexandria, VA: Association for Supervision and Curriculum Development.

Marzano, R., Pickering, D., & Pollack, J. (2004). Classroom instruction that works: Research-based strategies for increasing student achievement. Alexandria, VA: Association for Supervision and Curriculum Development.

Messick, S. (1989). Validity. In R. L. Linn (Ed.), *Educational measurement* (3rd ed., pp. 13–103). Phoenix, AZ: Oryx Press.

Nisbett, R., & Ross, L. (1980). *Human inference: Strategies and shortcomings of social judgment*. Englewood Cliffs, NJ: Prentice Hall.

Pashler, H., McDaniel, M., Rohrer, D., & Bjork, R. (2008). Learning styles concepts and evidence. *Psychological Science in the Public Interest, 9*, 105–119.

Schunk, D. H. (1996). Goal and self-evaluative influence during children's cognitive skill learning. *American Educational Research Journal, 24*, 359–382.

Seligman, M. (1990). A gifted ninth grader tells it like it is today. *Gifted Child Today 13*(4), 9–11.

Shulman, L. S. (1986). Paradigms and research programs in the study of teaching: A contemporary perspective. In M. C. Wittrock (Ed.), *Handbook of research on teaching* (3rd ed., pp. 3–36). New York: Macmillan.

Simmons, D. C., & Kame'enui, E. J. (1990). The effect of task alternatives on vocabulary knowledge: A comparison of students with and without learning disabilities. *Journal of Learning Disabilities, 23*, 291–297.

Smith, P. L. (1992, April). *A model for selection from supplantive and generative instructional strategies for problem-solving instruction*. Paper presented at the conference of the American Educational Research Association, San Francisco, CA.

Snider, V. (1992). Learning styles and learning to read: A critique. *Remedial and Special Education, 13*(1), 6–18.

Stahl, S. A., & Kuhn, M. R. (1995). Does whole language instruction matched to learning styles help children learn to read? *School Psychology Review, 24*, 393–404.

Stone, J. E. (1996). Developmentalism: An obscure but pervasive restriction on educational improvement. *Educational Policy Analysis Archives, 4*(8). Available at *http://epaa.asu.edu/ojs/article/view/631/753*.

Teddlie, C., Kirby, P. C., & Stringfield, S. (1989). Effective versus ineffective schools: Observable differences in the classroom. *American Journal of Education, 97*, 221–236.

Tobias, S. (1994). Interest, prior knowledge, and learning. *Review of Educational Research, 64*, 37–54.

Torgesen, J. K., Alexander, A. W., Wagner, R. K., Rashotte, C. A., Voeller, K. K. S., & Conway, T. (2001). Intensive remedial instruction for children with severe reading disabilities: Immediate and long-term outcomes from two instructional approaches. *Journal of Learning Disabilities, 34*(1), 33–58.

Ulman, J. D., & Rosenberg, M. S. (1986). Science and superstition in special education. *Exceptional Children, 52*, 459–460.

U.S. Department of Education, National Center for Education Statistics. (2012). *The condition of education 2012* (Publication No. NCES 2012-045). Washington, DC: U.S. Government Printing Office.

Vaughn, S., Linan-Thompson, S., & Hickman, P. (2003). Response to instruction as a means of identifying students with reading/learning disabilities. *Exceptional Children, 69*, 391–409.

Volpe, R., & Fabiano, G. (2013). *Daily behavior report cards: An evidence-based system of assessment and intervention*. New York: Guilford Press.

Vygotsky, L. (1978). *Mind in society: The development of higher psychological processes*. Cambridge, MA: Harvard University Press.

Waugh, R. P. (1975). The I.T.P.A.: Ballast or bonanza for the school psychologist? *Journal of School Psychology, 13*, 201–208.

Wanzek, J., & Vaughn, S. (2008). Response to varying amounts of time in reading intervention for students demonstrating insufficient response to intervention. *Journal of Learning Disabilities, 41*, 126–142.

Weinstein, C.E., & Mayer, R.F. (1986). The teaching of learning strategies. In M.C. Wittrock (Ed.), *Handbook of research on teaching* (pp. 315–327). New York: Macmillan.

Ysseldyke, J. E., Algozzine, R., & Thurlow, M. L. (2000). *Critical issues in special education*. Boston: Houghton Mifflin.

Index

An *f* following a page number indicates a figure; a *t* following a page number indicates a table; page numbers in **bold** refer to terms in the glossary.

Accomplishment, 32–33, **145**

Aggregating information, 70–73, 71*f*

Alignment, 6, 56, **145**

Alterable, **145**

Alterable variables, 9, 26–27, **145**

Approaches, teaching. *See* Instruction; Teaching approaches

Assessment. *See also* RIOT (Review, Interview, Observe, Test) assessment procedures; SCIL (Setting, Curriculum, Instruction, Learners) evaluation domains; Screening

   definition, **145**

   forms for, 134*f*

   overview, 3–4, 4*f*, 6–7

   phase 2 in the CBE inquiry process, 46–47, 85–89

   replication in, 86–89

Assessment instruments. *See* Instruments

Assessment questions, 4, **145**

Assumed causes. *See also* Causes

   definition, **145**

   overview, 76

   rules for developing, 77–83, 78*t*, 79*t*

   rules for testing, 83–85, 83*t*

   summarization and, 89–91

   troubleshooting and, 125–126

   verification, 90–91

Automaticity, 106–107, **145**

C

Causes. *See also* Assumed causes

   inquiry process and, 50

   phase 2 in the CBE inquiry process, 46–47, 76–83, 77*f*, 78*t*, 79*t*, 81*f*, 83–85, 83*t*

Classroom materials, 7, 28, 132

Classroom-level screening and intervention, 55–61, 57*f*, 58*f*, 60*f*, 131

Common Core State Standards (CCSS), 61, 95, 96

Concepts, 27, **145**. *See also* Knowledge

Content, 29–30, 131–132

Criterion of acceptable performance (CAP)

   definition, **145**

   goals and, 93–94

   overview, 63–64

   phase 3 in the CBE inquiry process, 100, 102*f*, 103*f*

   troubleshooting and, 119, 121

Criterion-referenced, 86, **146**

Curriculum

   CBE and, 6, 14–15

   definition, **146**

   overview, 28

   SCIL (Setting, Curriculum, Instruction, Learners) evaluation domains, 67–68, 69*f*

   supplantive teaching approaches and, 36–37

Curriculum derived, 7, **146**

Curriculum independent, 7, **146**

Curriculum-based assessment (CBA), 5, 5*f*, 7, **146**

Curriculum-based assessment for instructional design (CBA-ID), 7

Curriculum-based evaluation overview, 1–2, 5–7, 14–15, 139, 140–143

   advantages of CBE, 10

   CBM and, 8–9

   definition, **146**

   developing a plan for using CBE, 130–136, 134*f*

   frequently asked questions regarding, 138–139

   hints on implementing and maintaining, 136–137

   problem solving and, 11

   resources, 153–155

   terminology associated with CBE, 3–5, 4*f*, 5*f*

   who uses CBE, 10

Curriculum-based measurement (CBM)
    CBE and, 8–9
    definition, **146**
    overview, 5, 5*f*, 8
    phase 3 in the CBE inquiry process, 105

D

Data, **146**
Data collection. *See also* Screening
    CBE and, 9
    developing a plan for using CBE, 133–135, 134*f*
    forms for, 134*f*
    overview, 7
    phase 1 in the CBE inquiry process, 45, 56
    progress monitoring, 114
    troubleshooting and, 116
Data poor, **146**
Data rich, **146**
Dead-man test, 62, 62*t*, 128*f*, **146**
Decision, 4–5, **146**
Decision fatigue, 10, **146**
Decision making. *See also* Formative decision making;
    Summative decision making
    CBE and, 5–7, 14
    compared to judgment, 20–24, 23*f*, 24*t*
    diagnostic decisions, 75–76
    phase 1 in the CBE inquiry process, 44–46, 68–70, 69*f*
    phase 2 in the CBE inquiry process, 46–47, 75
    phase 3 in the CBE inquiry process, 48–49
    valuing data and evidence and, 24–25
Diagnostic decisions, 75–76, **146**
Differentiated instruction, 55, **147**
Disconfirming evidence, 70–73, 71*f*, **147**

E

Effect size, 97, **147**
Empirically derived, 64, **147**
Evaluation. *See also* RIOT (Review, Interview, Observe, Test)
    assessment procedures; SCIL (Setting, Curriculum,
    Instruction, Learners) evaluation domains
    definition, **147**
    domains of, 67–68
    overview, 4, 4*f*
    phase 1 in the CBE inquiry process and, 52
Evidence, 21, **147**
Evidence based, 14, **147**
Experts, 21–22, **147**

F

Fact finding, 16, 134*f*. *See also* Phase 1 in the CBE inquiry
    process
F.AC.T.R. acronym (Fact–Assumed Cause–Test–Result)
    forms for, 134*f*
    instructional design and, 96

    overview, 80–83, 81*f*
    summarization and, 89–91
    troubleshooting and, 125–126
Facts, 27, **147**. *See also* Knowledge
Feedback, 101, 102*f*, 103*f*, 121
Fidelity of implementation
    forms for, 115*f*, 120*f*
    progress monitoring, 114
    troubleshooting and, 112–113, 118–121, 120*f*
Focus of instruction/intervention. *See also* Instruction
    definition, **147**
    developing a plan for using CBE, 131–132
    forms for, 123*f*
    overview, 95, 95*f*, 96
    troubleshooting and, 124
Format of instruction/intervention. *See also* Instruction
    definition, **147**
    forms for, 123*f*
    overview, 95, 95*f*, 96
    troubleshooting and, 124
Formative assessment, 11–12, **147**
Formative decision making, 17, 48–49, 92. *See also*
    Decision making; Instruction; Instructional planning;
    Phase 3 in the CBE inquiry process
Frequency of instruction/intervention. *See also*
    Instruction
    definition, **147**
    forms for, 123*f*
    overview, 95, 95*f*, 96
    phase 3 in the CBE inquiry process, 111
    progress monitoring, 105–106
    troubleshooting and, 122, 124

G

General outcome measure (GOM), 9, 105, 106*t*, **147**
Generative approach, **147**
Generative teaching method, 34–38, 35*t*, 38*t*. *See also*
    Instruction
Glossary, **147**
Goal line
    definition, **148**
    overview, 109, 109*t*
    troubleshooting and, 114, 116
Goals
    definition, **148**
    for each lesson, 98–99, 102*f*, 103*f*, 119
    phase 3 in the CBE inquiry process, 48, 93–94
Grade level, 131
Graphing student performance
    developing a plan for using CBE, 135–136
    phase 3 in the CBE inquiry process, 106–111, 108*f*,
    109*f*, 110*f*
    troubleshooting and, 114–118, 115*f*, 117*f*

H

Heuristic overlay, 10, **148**

I

Individualized assessment, 4, **148**. *See also* Assessment
Individualized instruction, 4, **148**. *See also* Instruction
Inference, 21, 24–25, **148**
Information, **148**
Information collection. *See* Data collection
Inquiry procedures. *See also* Phase 1 in the CBE inquiry
    process; Phase 2 in the CBE inquiry process; Phase 3
    in the CBE inquiry process
    CBE process of, 5–7, 9, 13, 41–44, 42*f*
    frequently asked questions regarding, 138–139
    hints on implementing and maintaining, 136–137
    overview, 41
    phase 1 overview, 41–42, 44–46
    phase 2 overview, 42, 46–47
    phase 3 overview, 42, 48–49
    troubleshooting, 49–50
Instruction. *See also* Formative decision making;
    Instructional design; Instructional planning
    CBE and, 6, 14–15
    definition, **148**
    developing a plan for using CBE, 130–136, 134*f*
    fidelity of implementation, 112–113
    implementing, 98–102, 102*f*, 103*f*, 118–121, 120*f*,
      130–136, 134*f*
    inquiry process and, 50
    misconceptions that influence learning and teaching,
      31–34
    phase 3 in the CBE inquiry process, 48
    SCIL (Setting, Curriculum, Instruction, Learners)
      evaluation domains, 67–68, 69*f*
    teaching approaches, 34–38, 35*t*, 38*t*, 39–40
Instructional design. *See also* Instruction
    inquiry process and, 50
    phase 3 in the CBE inquiry process, 48, 94–98, 95*f*
    troubleshooting and, 122–124, 123*f*
Instructional planning. *See also* Formative decision
    making; Instruction
    CBA-ID, 7
    CBE and, 6
    developing a plan for using CBE, 130–136, 134*f*
    phase 1 in the CBE inquiry process, 56
    phase 3 in the CBE inquiry process, 93–94
Instruments. *See also* Assessment
    definition, **148**
    overview, 4
    phase 2 in the CBE inquiry process, 85–89
    phase 3 in the CBE inquiry process, 104–105
    progress monitoring and, 118
Intervention. *See also* Instruction
    CBE and, 14–15
    designing, 94–98, 95*f*
    developing a plan for using CBE, 130–136, 134*f*
    fidelity of implementation, 112–113
    implementing, 118–121, 120*f*, 130–136, 134*f*
    need for early intervention, 141
Interview assessment, **148**. *See also* Assessment; RIOT
    (Review, Interview, Observe, Test) assessment
    procedures; Screening

J

Judgment
    compared to decision making, 20–24, 23*f*, 24*t*
    definition, **148**
    valuing data and evidence and, 24–25

K

Knowledge, 27–31. *See also* Prior knowledge

L

Learned helplessness, 33, **148**
Learner, 67–68, 69*f*, **148**
Learning, 25–26, 27, 39–40, 142
Learning orientation, 33, **148**
Learning preferences, 34, **149**
Learning problems
    overview, 141
    phase 1 in the CBE inquiry process, 44–45, 55–64, 57*f*,
      58*f*, 59*f*, 60*f*, 62*t*
    teaching approaches and, 37–38, 38*t*, 39
Learning styles, 34, **149**
Learning targets, 93–94, **149**. *See also* Goals

M

Mastery
    assumed causes and, 77–79, 78*t*, 79*t*
    phase 2 in the CBE inquiry process, 76–77
    phase 3 in the CBE inquiry process, 101–102, 102*f*,
      103*f*
    summarization and, 89–91
    teaching approaches and, 38*t*
Mastery measures, 7, 104–105, 106*t*, **149**
Materials. *See* Classroom materials; Curriculum
Measurement, 3, **149**
Measurement drift, 104, **149**
Memorization, 28
Metacognition, 27, 30–31, **149**. *See also* Knowledge
Monitoring of progress. *See* Progress monitoring
Motivation, 32–33, 38*t*, **149**
Multi-tier systems of supports (MTSS), 12–13, 141, **149**

N

Norm reference instruments, 7, **149**

O

Objectives. *See also* Goals
    definition, **149**
    for each lesson, 98–99, 102*f*, 103*f*, 119
    phase 3 in the CBE inquiry process, 93–94